THE
DRUNKEN
SILENUS

THE DRUNKEN SILENUS

On Gods, Goats,
and the Cracks in Reality

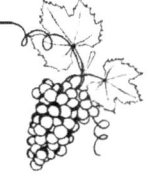

MORGAN MEIS

SL/\NT
BOOKS

THE DRUNKEN SILENUS
On Gods, Goats, and the Cracks in Reality

Copyright © 2020 Morgan Meis. All rights reserved. Except
for brief quotations in critical publications or reviews, no part
of this book may be reproduced in any manner without prior
written permission from the publisher. Write: Permissions,
Slant Books P.O. Box 60295, Seattle, WA 98160.

Slant Books
P.O. Box 60295
Seattle, WA 98160

www.slantbooks.com

HARDCOVER ISBN: 978-1-63982-055-9
PAPERBACK ISBN: 978-1-63982-054-2
EBOOK ISBN: 978-1-63982-056-6

Cataloguing-in-Publication data:

Names: Meis, Morgan.

Title: The drunken Silenus : On gods, goats, and the cracks in
    reality / Morgan Meis.

Description: Seattle, WA: Slant Books, 2020.

Identifiers: ISBN 978-1-63982-055-9 (hardcover) | ISBN 978-1-
    63982-054-2 (paperback) | ISBN 978-1-63982-056-6 (ebook)

Subjects: LCSH: Rubens, Peter Paul -- 1577-1640 | Mythology,
    Classical, in literature | Greek drama (Tragedy) -- History
    and criticism.

Classification: ND673.R9 M45 2020(print) | ND673.R9 (ebook)

Manufactured in the U.S.A.   OCTOBER 12, 2021

For Shuffy and Matthew Power

Contents

Preface

I STARTED WRITING THIS BOOK WHILE living in Antwerp. I was there because my wife, the indefatigable Shuffy, was making a short film ostensibly centering on Abraham Ortelius, the great cartographer and man-about-Antwerp circa the mid to late sixteenth century. We were also rapidly spending a not insignificant chunk of change I'd managed to wheedle from the Andy Warhol Foundation for my writings on art and what-not. Problem was, I had no particular project to be doing in Antwerp, other than cooking for Shuffy and tending to her needs, a not unpleasant commission but, then again, it is said that idle hands are the devil's workshop and there is, indeed, some wisdom in the saying. Suddenly, or so it seems to me now, I remembered that Antwerp was, among other things, Peter Paul Rubens's town. This thought annoyed me, since I had absolutely no interest in Rubens. I didn't even care about him enough to dislike him. My next thought was, "I'll write a book about Rubens."

It pleased me to write about Rubens since my lack of interest allowed me to focus on developing a new way of writing about art, new to me at least. There are others who've attempted something similar. But not too many, I'd wager. I was working on a style. The style would be direct, sometimes even downright agitated in nature. I wanted it to be funny and strange. I wanted it to be shamelessly intellectual at times and shamelessly crude at others. I wanted this style to be able to touch on deep things, profound problems of being alive, but also to let those problems hang unresolved, to raise issues of some import and then also to laugh at them. I wanted to create a style that would unfold in spirals rather than in lines.

I hope I've succeeded to some degree. I'll let others be the ultimate judges. That's how it always is anyway. I came, I should mention, to feel quite strongly about Rubens in the end. I came to recognize that he was a real artist, whatever exactly that means. But it must mean, at least, that he wrangled with the hardest things both in terms of his craft, the medium, and in terms of what you can do, what you can show through that medium.

I believe that this little book can be read with some amusement by those who will allow themselves to be so amused, and, I might add, *plus uno maneat perenne saeclo*.

1. Rubens discovers Titian, who had already discovered Silenus . . . but who is Silenus?

EARLY IN HIS ADULT LIFE, PETER PAUL Rubens, the famous painter—though he was not yet famous at the time—took a trip to Italy with his apprentice Deodat del Monte. Rubens had been living in Antwerp with his mother. He wasn't born in Antwerp, he was born in Siegen, in what is now Germany but was, at the time, not the unified country that it is today. Rubens was born in the time before nation-states as we know them existed. Before the French Revolution, before Bismarck, before Napoleon. Rubens was born in Siegen because his father had been in prison there, or thereabouts. That's another part of the story we'll get into later, the arrest and near execution of Rubens's father. Rubens's mother moved back to Antwerp after the death of that man, her husband, Peter Paul Rubens's father, Jan Rubens. They couldn't live in Antwerp while Jan Rubens was alive because he wasn't allowed to go back to Antwerp. Nobody wanted to see him around there. He wasn't welcome. But then Jan died and Rubens and his brother

Philip and the other children moved back to Antwerp with their mother. And Rubens grew up from the age of ten or so until his early twenties as an Antwerp boy.

Antwerp was an important city then, but past its prime. Antwerp is in Belgium now, but that would have made no sense to the people of Antwerp at the time of Rubens since there was no such place as Belgium then. When Rubens was alive, Antwerp was thought of primarily as a place in Flanders. This is the late sixteenth century into the early seventeenth century. Antwerp was at its greatest during the mid-sixteenth century, when its port brought in goods from all over the world and its printing houses printed the most important books and its prominent citizens built structures and institutions of prominence. That did not last very long, mostly because of the religious wars and the pressures that were pulling the Hapsburg Empire apart. The great prominence of Antwerp didn't last very long at all, a generation or two, and then the city fades back into history as a secondary place.

So, Rubens took a trip to Italy. Then, as now, Italy was beautiful and then, as now, people were attracted to that beauty. Plus, Rubens was a painter and all the great painters were in Italy at that time. If you were a painter, you were interested in Italy.

The Italy sojourn interests us most for the simple reason that Titian was in Italy. Titian was dead, of course, before Rubens ever got to Venice. But the paintings were there. We know that Rubens looked at the paintings and that he was moved by the paintings.

I'm reasonably certain that Rubens was amazed and astounded by one Titian in particular. That painting is today called *Bacchus and Ariadne*. The narrative of that painting is focused on those two figures. Bacchus is the name that the Romans gave to the Greek god Dionysus, often referred to as the God of Wine, though that makes him seem like the god of dinner parties which, you can be sure, is very far indeed from the real significance of Bacchus/Dionysus. Ariadne is a mythological figure who you will remember as the daughter of King Minos of Crete. Ariadne helped Theseus defeat the Minotaur and then to find his way out of the labyrinth. Ariadne gave Theseus a thread, which he unwound in order to find his way back out of the labyrinth, and that is why you will still hear, today, the phrase "Ariadne's thread" referred to as a way to get out of difficulties. In the old stories, Ariadne runs off with Theseus after he defeats the Minotaur but is then, in turn, abandoned by Theseus on the island of Naxos. That is where she meets Bacchus/Dionysus. He comes to her on the island of Naxos and takes her for his bride. This is the moment that Titian is treating in his famous painting. Later, in many of the stories, we are told that Ariadne hangs herself from a tree. But that happens later.

In the painting, Ariadne has her back to us and seems in the early stages of flight from Bacchus and his motley crew. They are, indeed, a rough bunch. Leopards lead the way, followed closely by a group of drunken fools and semi-humans. Satyrs dance about on their goat legs. The Dionysian ladies, the Maenads, pound on cymbals and tambourines. A severed cow head is dragged along on a rope by a wicked-looking baby satyr. A rough bunch. Ariadne is, wisely, looking for an exit route. But Bacchus leaps from his chariot in a flowing red cape to intercede. The painting catches him in mid-leap. There, suspended in the air, Bacchus is a miracle. He might as well be coming down directly from the heavens. Look at his face. Look at the rapture.

But our real interest is in the background of the painting. There he is in the top right, in the back, just coming on to the scene. It is the fat man. He rides an ass. His head lolls to the left. He's in a stupor again. Silenus. Poor Silenus.

That fat man, Silenus, has been following Bacchus/Dionysus around from the very beginning. Part hostage, part acolyte, we hear from the Homeric hymns of old that Silenus was a tutor to the young god. He was born to a nymph or, depending on who you ask, sprung directly from the earth. Silenus attends to Bacchus—that is his role. He tries to keep up with the party. But he is a wreck. It is too much for him. The other attendants to Bacchus hold him up as the ass tramps from one gathering to another. Silenus takes another drink.

In his own painting career, Rubens was to develop a minor obsession with Silenus. It is almost as if Rubens plucked Silenus right out of Titian's painting and made him a star in his own right. It is as if there, in the background of Titian's painting, Rubens saw something important that he couldn't let go. Rubens wanted to run with some truth of which Titian had gotten a glimpse.

* * *

It's possible, of course, that Rubens never saw that painting by Titian at all. Maybe Rubens read about Silenus somewhere else, perusing the Orphic hymns in some leather-bound volume. Rubens liked to think of himself as a classicist. He would have had leather-bound volumes lying around his studio. Note, for instance, that ridiculous little vignette, that puff piece by Otto Sperling, the doctor to the Danish king and, presumably, one of the top sycophants of his time. Otto visited Rubens in his studio and wrote the following, "the master was working on a canvas while listening to a reading of Tacitus and simultaneously dictating a letter. Since we did not dare interrupt him, he himself addressed us, while continuing to paint, listen to the reading, and dictate his letter." Why not mention that Rubens was frying an egg and teaching his dog to speak while he was at it?

Who knows how or when Rubens first came across Silenus? Still, I prefer to think of Rubens being struck dumb while looking at that painting by Titian. Who is that wrecked man riding the ass in the back of the scene, he would have wondered. All the fancy activity in the foreground of Titian's painting was suddenly forgotten in place of the pitiful scene of Silenus on his ass. That's the truth of the whole scene, Rubens must have thought. Silenus rides in silent judgment of the whole affair. Silenus knows that the whole crazy circus is just for show. Behind it all is the base fact that life has no meaning.

* * *

I'll tell you one thing about that Silenus Titian painted in his *Bacchus and Ariadne*. He is so very tired and so very fat. A fatter more tired man has never been captured via pigment. He's asleep, or in a stupor at least. He's utterly oblivious to all the action happening at the other side of the painting, with Bacchus's leaping about and Ariadne's forestalled flight from the canvas. Another member of Bacchus's retinue seems to be holding Silenus up as he droops off the ass he is riding. Maybe the man or satyr holding Silenus up is also whispering something into his right ear, it is impossible to say for sure.

If Titian's Silenus is ever having any fun, he isn't doing it here. But this is the Silenus you can imagine uttering his famous words of wisdom. This is the Silenus that jumped up out of that painting and struck Rubens dumbfounded. This Silenus spoke to Rubens. We can presume that Silenus said the same thing to Rubens that he said to King Midas in the old myth. In the Greek myths, King Midas went looking for Silenus. He'd heard that Silenus was hiding a bit of wisdom and he wanted to hear what it was. He captured the drunken fat man. How hard could it be? He offered Silenus some wine. He replaced the water of a spring with delightful hooch and Silenus couldn't leave. What's the secret?

King Midas asked. What's this thing you know? What's the best thing for man?

The secret, Silenus said, is that it would have been better not to have been born at all. The next best thing for man, Silenus added, would be to die quickly.

2. The forgotten city of Antwerp and some speculation as to why Rubens felt at home there. Perhaps it all has to do with a lingering melancholy.

RUBENS BUILT HIS HOUSE IN ANTWERP. It is a strange place, that house. That strange man built a Venetian palazzo in Flanders. It is not a Venetian palazzo, exactly. It has the elements of a Venetian palazzo. But it has the outward façade of the comfortable home of a Flemish burgher. Then it breaks out into Venetian exuberance on the inside. Even on the inside the exuberance comes and goes. In some parts of the house, the design calms down and gets Northern European again. Then, out near the gardens it erupts into arches and statuary. Back and forth. It is a rumbly bumbly ride walking through that house. Some of the rooms are dark like tombs, brown to their very soul. Dark brown wombs where a person could huddle away for an entire winter season. These seem like rooms for forgetting. But maybe they are rooms for remembering, rooms for whiling the hours away in contemplation of the past. Either way, they are rooms of the interior. And then the inner façades and courtyards of the house present another celebration. So, the outward face of the building is in the mode of a comfortable burgher. These lead the way into the dark and brooding rooms of brown and browner. And these rooms open up to the courtyards that make a Venetian show.

The thing Rubens really wanted, then, was to hide his Venetian joy. You could walk by that house all your life and never know that there is a flower inside. You could walk into the house and drop off some ducks in the kitchen and never know. There are a hundred ways you could experience that house and never know. Rubens liked that idea. He liked the idea that his burgher's house was the hiding place for a palazzo. He wrapped his palazzo up in a dirty bag and then hid it in plain sight, right in the middle of Antwerp, a dead city when he lived there. He wanted to walk around a dead city as its most prominent ghost, his own secret.

Why was Antwerp a dead city, for ghosts? Because the bastards silted up the river, of course. The men from Holland washed their hands of the entire city in exactly 1585. Oh, they closed the river up alright, they dumped the earth into the Scheldt until Antwerp couldn't be a harbor anymore. Then they went back to reading tracts of Calvinist theology and making money. They had stopped the Spanish and the Counter Reformation right there in Antwerp. This is all in the history books. I can't explain it all to you. There was a Reformation and a Counter Reformation. There were Orangemen and Hapsburgs and always the French lurking in the background. There were matters of politics and matters of religion. The guys up North, the men from Holland, said to Antwerp, in essence, you can have your sandy river and your Pope too. You can have your bloated, dying church. You can have your Hapsburg potentates. We'll just move all the commerce up to Amsterdam and begin the task of forgetting you. And there were wars and there were killings. The people of Antwerp were roused from slumber more than once and dragged into the streets to be butchered by one group or another.

And that is where Rubens spent the second half of his life. He roamed the ghost city of the Counter Reformation watching it all die, watching the city dry up and flake away into the wind. He built his secret palazzo and settled in for the decline. Maybe he even liked it that way. Maybe he thought it was funny, or just true. He could be the last man in the city of death.

3. King Midas's dilemma and the disappointing nature of Silenus's so-called wisdom. What if wisdom isn't what we think it is?

OLD KING MIDAS CAN'T HAVE BEEN pleased when he heard the wisdom of Silenus. In the old stories, he doesn't do anything at all, the king. He just lets Silenus go. The stories don't mention anything about stunned silence, but it is easy to imagine the stunned silence, and then the anger. The king would have acted quickly to protect his own mind from the so-called wisdom of Silenus. This fat clown has lost his way, Midas would have told himself. This fat clown is only trying to trick me, or he never possessed any wisdom in the first place. The king would have convinced himself to forget about Silenus and keep moving. What other choice does a king have? A king is committed, if nothing else, to living, to moving on with all the earthly business. A king, even in his cynicism, must believe in, if nothing else, his own manipulations. He would have killed Silenus right there on the spot if he could have. But kings are usually tactful enough not to try to kill the friends of the gods. Instead,

Midas let Silenus go and then turned his attention to other secrets and finally to the secret of gold. And that too was a disappointment, that too was the opposite of what it promised to be. King Midas, it seems, was not one to take the hint. He kept going until it ruined him. He turned everything he loved into gold and killed everything that mattered.

In many of the tales, it is Dionysus (Bacchus) who gives Midas his power of golden touch. King Midas, in all his anger and disappointment at the so-called wisdom of Silenus, sees an angle after all. He realizes that Dionysus is probably fond of his drunken fat man, the old man who tutored him so dutifully for all those years. King Midas sees that returning Silenus to the god will put him in a good light. Perhaps he will enjoy the favor of the god.

And King Midas was right. Dionysus is happy that Midas returned to him his beloved drunken tutor, Silenus. He does bestow upon King Midas a special gift. He gives to Midas an amazing power, the long-dreamt-of power to turn things into gold. The power to make everything, everything in the world, into gold.

Over time, Midas realizes that his power of the golden touch is a mixed blessing. Then he comes to realize it is a curse. Maybe the king starts to appreciate the blessing of death around that time, starts to see a little glimmer of what Silenus was talking about. Maybe not.

Later in the tale, Midas manages to get the power of the golden touch taken away and becomes a follower of

Pan. He moves back to the forest with a group of satyrs and forest beasts. He is looking for something, still. Old Midas is sure that a great wisdom, a final truth, must be lurking out in the woods with the half-men and the drunks, with the wild Dionysian frenzies. He can't stay away. He loves the shrill flute music of Pan so much that he values it above the music of Apollo. Apollo's music is the glorious music of a real god, not the sounds of a shrunken goat man playing on a flute. But Midas can't stand the music of Apollo. It is not the wild music of the forest. Apollo is annoyed. He is contemptuous of the ears of King Midas, with his inability to listen. King Midas never did listen very well. He couldn't hear what he needed to hear from Silenus and he cannot hear the music properly either. The sounds going into his ears never make their way properly into his understanding. Apollo is disgusted with Midas's inability to make distinctions between what is great and what is merely the wild noise of the forest, the drunken music of foolishness and revelry. So Apollo gives Midas a pair of donkey ears. That's what you get, Apollo says, when you listen like an ass. And that is what Midas got for wanting to know something, for falling in love with the wild sounds and the bestial mingling of the forest gods, the drunken gods. He went looking for Silenus's wisdom and he wound up part donkey.

The question is, did old King Midas hear something after all?

* * *

Silenus is hardly a primary figure after that. Ovid tells his story. He crops up in vase paintings and other such places. He lingers at the margins. He recedes, mostly, into the mists of mythology and folklore. Then, in the sixteenth century Titian notices Silenus again. He turns a little bit of his painterly attention to Silenus, indulging an interest in the Dionysian characters that fascinated him for whatever painterly reason. Titian wanted to show us all the leaping glory of Dionysus in the moment he makes Ariadne his own. To do so, he wanted to show the whole Dionysian entourage, the entire mad affair making its way through the forest. The city is far in the distance. The normal affairs of men play not a role in this zone. This is the zone of Dionysus. This is the zone of unexplainable life.

And there, in the back, Titian chose to include Silenus in the procession. And more importantly, he chose to paint Silenus as the very essence of tired and fat. He chose to paint Silenus in the state of barely holding on. He chose to paint Silenus as carrying a terrible burden. And that was the image that struck our friend Rubens and stayed with him over the years. That was the image of Silenus that lingered in the brain of Rubens, imprinting him.

Maybe.

Rubens thought, surely, this is the Silenus that makes sense. The Silenus who told King Midas that the best thing is not to have been born at all would be a man engaged in the act of forgetting. If that is the one big thought, the one truth that you have to offer, then even your moments of gaiety are going to be characterized by despair. Your clowning is going to be weighed down by the immensity of that thought. We are assuming here that Silenus was telling King Midas the truth. Titian's painting proceeds under that assumption. It proceeds from the idea that Silenus was a wrecked man who would, in fact, say exactly what he said to King Midas. Titian proceeds as if his Silenus was the type of man/god who, captured by Midas, would give in to the request, and would reveal his one piece of essential wisdom as a thought of utter despair.

That's what Rubens saw in Titian's painting. Silenus, and the truth of Silenus. And in seeing that, he was never able to paint scenes of Dionysus without the truth of Silenus being right there at the forefront. In fact, Rubens went even further. He went on to depict Dionysus in the light of Silenus, and not the other way round. Rubens's painting of Dionysus (Bacchus) from the late 1630s is not the lithe and leaping Dionysus of Titian's imagination. Dionysus, the way Rubens paints him, is lumbering and fat, just like Silenus. He is overburdened with flesh. This is not the boy-god of the ancients, the figure of an ever-renewable, seasonal life force. The Dionysus that Rubens painted, years after he had seen that Titian painting in Venice, has been completely Silenusized. The other possible meanings of Dionysus have dropped away.

We are left with Silenus as the truth of Dionysus.

4. Thinking about Silenus leads unavoidably to thinking about Nietzsche, which, unexpectedly, links an artist and a philosopher not otherwise often linked. Is this mere coincidence?

RUBENS PAINTED HIS GREAT SILENUS painting sometime before 1620, maybe as early as 1615. He brought Silenus to the forefront of the painting, as the primary figure. There are other figures in the painting. But, basically, it is a painting of Silenus and no one else. Rubens is painting Silenus for the sole reason of painting the truth of Silenus.

There is nothing clownish about the Silenus that Rubens painted. Silenus is a serious character. He is stumbling forward with that look of confused determination that only a profoundly drunk person can have. Silenus is surrounded by the same group of satyrs, revelers, wild beasts, and maniacs that we've come to know from Titian's painting. They are heckling the old man as he stumbles forward.

I don't know if you've ever been that drunk before. I have. You jump up suddenly because you've got to get somewhere. Maybe you just want to go home, you need to get home. But you don't really know where you are. More troubling, you aren't even sure who you are. But a thought, a need has taken hold of you and it is the only thing with any stability. It is a sharp pang of reality in a world that has otherwise lost its bearings. You stumble forward in that specific oblivion. There is a clarity in that oblivion, but it is the clarity of oblivion.

In the painting, a black man, one of the members of the Dionysian retinue, stands behind Silenus and pinches a chunk of skin just beneath his left butt cheek. He is pinching the skin quite hard. But Silenus doesn't even seem to notice. His brain, awash in alcohol, can only focus on one thing, and barely that. He has to get home, or wherever. He has to move forward.

Why was Rubens so interested in this fat, drunken man? Why did he feel the need to pull Silenus up and out of Titian's famous painting?

* * *

We must speak of Nietzsche, now. If we are going to continue to speak about Silenus, then we are going to have to bring Nietzsche into the picture. Nietzsche, the terrible German. There is no way around it, alas. He's the only man in several thousand years, the only man other than Rubens to have sniffed out the real importance of Silenus. He did it around two hundred years after Rubens. But he did it for the same reason. He saw that the story of Silenus exposed a side of the ancient Greeks that people were not talking about. He became obsessed with the truth of Silenus.

Nietzsche was born in Röcken on the afternoon of October fifteenth in the year of our Lord 1844. Twenty-seven or so years into his life, Nietzsche wrote his first book, which he called *The Birth of Tragedy*. It was a simple book.

Nietzsche decided that the Silenus story was central. If you understand the Silenus story, he said, then you understand much of what was driving the Greeks to make tragedy, this new art form. What are these Greeks up to with their tragedies? Nietzsche wondered. What is it with these Dionysian rites and the dancing of the goats? He could smell an essential truth, could Nietzsche. He wanted every thought to be a bomb. This is different from Rubens. Rubens painted difficult subjects with honesty, but he didn't necessarily like it. He did not want, necessarily, to break people's heads open. Rubens wasn't a malicious painter. Mischievous sometimes, maybe, but not malicious, not destructive. He wasn't obsessed with making explosions. Rubens always tried to muffle the blast.

But Nietzsche was different. He was crazy. He was crazy from the beginning and he got crazier over time. By the end he was certifiably insane, raving mad as they used to say. *The Birth of Tragedy* is his best work because he had the crazy under some control. He could let it out in bursts. His thoughts had some time to develop in those early days. Later, he stopped caring. His crazy took complete control. No one should read *Twilight of the Idols.* It is an obscene act to read that work. It is just looking in on another man's mental dissolution. There is nothing there.

But in *The Birth of Tragedy*, the genius hasn't gone under yet. The figure of Silenus rises up out of that work and speaks to us exactly as Rubens would have envisioned it. It is the Silenus of Rubens's painting that speaks in Nietzsche's work. It is that specific Silenus, the one that Rubens rescued from the background of Titian's painting and restored to his full Greek strangeness. The drunk staggering across the scene with the pinching satyrs cackling along at his side. That Silenus, on the move, barely able to remember who he is. Rubens and Nietzsche would have understood one another about that.

All this talk (Nietzsche realized) of the measured and balanced Greek mind was sloppy. No, there is turmoil. Nietzsche saw it because he was willing to look. He didn't listen to anybody else, the experts, the other scholars. He just took a look. He made himself into a scholar so that he could take a look on his own. Nietzsche saw something awful and essential. He saw a root sense of life that bubbled and boiled to no specific purpose. The sheer drive of existence. The sheer expression of a life drive and a death drive. Even that doesn't explain it very well. It is hard to give words to the thing that Nietzsche saw, the mad, empty discharge of life spoke to him out of that ancient Greek tragic sense, the one that produced the tragedies. The one that celebrated Dionysian rites in secret caves. The one that pulled animals apart with its bare hands. The one that had the voice of a goat, the bleat of a goat.

* * *

From what I know about Nietzsche's life, he never went to Antwerp. I don't think he would have liked the city. But Nietzsche didn't like any of the cities he lived in. Nietzsche was in the perennially unsatisfied category of persons. He would change the geography frequently, supposing that the change would improve his mood. We've all done this. If I could just get out of x and get to y, we think, then everything would be better. Some of us will stumble upon the insight that the trouble is, perhaps, being carried around on the inside. Nietzsche was carrying his troubles around on the inside and no act of geographical transformation, no circumlocution was going to change that fact. Probably, though, Nietzsche was already too crazy, even at the time he was writing *The Birth of Tragedy*, to come to any such self-realization.

If Nietzsche had been a different man, he could have learned something from our friend Rubens. Rubens decided, after some youthful travels, that he'd just go ahead and stay in Antwerp. It was obvious to Rubens and everybody else at the time that Antwerp was on the downward slide. The Dutch bastards had silted up the river. The Spanish troops garrisoning in the city had, not so long ago, whipped themselves into paroxysms of anger about not getting paid and started randomly slaughtering the citizens of Antwerp. Truly. It was in the late sixteenth century one day. The Spanish troops just up and slaughtered several thousand people, maybe around six, seven thousand people. That was the kind of thing going on in Antwerp when Rubens decided, not long afterward, that this was the city for him. This place was as good a place as any to settle down for good. They cleaned up the dead bodies and that was enough for Rubens. He was staying.

Rubens had learned a lesson that Nietzsche was never quite able to get through his head. It doesn't matter. It just doesn't matter where you do it, where you live out your life. If the shit inside is solid then it will never matter. Alas, as we've already noted, the shit inside Nietzsche was anything but solid. It was runny.

They both found themselves smack against the figure of Silenus, though. They both became Silenus men—Nietzsche pulling himself back on the thread of the ancient texts, Rubens following the images, diving into the painting by Titian and discovering the true Silenus there.

5. We sometimes think of Greek
   Tragedy as a refined affair, but it
   had its origins in a nasty, bawdy
   business.

NIETZSCHE DID SOMETHING VERY
SIMPLE when he wrote *The Birth of Tragedy*.
He asked himself a clear question, "What is
the Dionysian?" and then he attempted to answer that
question. His answer was that the Dionysian is a feeling
of ecstatic oneness with the surrounding universe.
That is why it is drunken and orgiastic. It is a losing of
oneself. With Dionysus, you merge with the one pure
life force. This is ecstasy. It is also a source of profound
depression when you come back. You realize, after an
orgiastic ecstasy, that your particular individuality does
not matter. You would rather be erased in the complete
cosmic overabundance. That's what happened with
Silenus. He had a taste of this drunken dissolution in
the One. It made him stop caring. It made him say to
King Midas that the best thing for any man is not to
have been born at all. The second best thing would be
to die quickly. Never living at all means never facing
the profound disappointment of being. It means never

We sometimes think of Greek Tragedy as a refined affair

experiencing the pain of being an individual when all that matters is the whole.

The Greeks gave an entire art form to that thought, to that feeling of root despair that comes along with the embrace of real life. That's the way Nietzsche saw it. Tragedy—the particular form of Greek tragedy—starts with the bleating of the goats and the wild shit going on in the Dionysian forest.

It's all there in the satyr plays. Jaunty numbers, the satyr plays were like festival entertainment. People would dress up like goats and tell dirty stories and run around the stage making lewd jokes. These festivals go back to the beginning, the harvest, the celebrations around another season of life. The Greek tragedies go back there. The satyr plays were part of the overall entertainment. The Greeks would set up scenarios where everybody was screwing everybody else and the whole lot of them would be very drunk.

There's no point putting a fine veneer on any of this. It was rough and it was nasty. It all came from the secret rites and the cultic behavior around Dionysus. These were harvest celebrations and they smelled of the earth. If you want to get a sense of what the satyr plays were all about the first thing you should do is take off all your clothes and then go outside into the country somewhere and roll around in the dirt screaming and crying. Then you'll be getting into the proper mood. Drink a liter of rot-gut whisky, foul stuff, the stuff that comes in plastic containers and has the word "Ol" in its brand name. Drink a liter of that while you are rolling around in the dirt and then get a few of your friends to punch you in the face while everyone chants the same phrase, whatever phrase you like, over and over again for about an hour. Then drink some more whisky and piss on yourself. Now you are ready to fuck the bare earth. Just hump away in the dirt. Try to fuck the actual earth, the core of her.

Now you're in the mood to understand a satyr play. Now you're in the mood to hang around with Silenus. Indeed, if you actually go through with this whole plan he may show up. If anything could actually bring Silenus, today, out of his hiding and into the fields of Pennsylvania, or wherever you are going to do this, it would be the above-described behavior. I do believe you'd have a chance at meeting the man/demigod in the flesh, the illustrious and wretched Silenus.

* * *

It bothers me, looking at that drunken Silenus painting by Rubens. The drunken Silenus in Titian's painting is bad enough. He teeters sadly, riding on his ass. He is a broken old man who can barely stay awake, barely stay conscious. But Rubens takes Silenus a thousand times more seriously. He paints Silenus with complete sincerity.

Silenus is a large man, the way Rubens imagines him. He is fat, of course. His youth is behind him, though not so far behind that his bushy beard has lost its color. He is wearing a pathetic, half-considered wreath. Probably one of the nasty satyrs nearby stuck it on his head as a joke. He's balding under that decrepit wreath and his side locks are going gray. Remember that the mortal status of Silenus is ambiguous from the beginning. He is one of those mid-category, half-human sorts. Born of the earth, born of a goddess, born of something not entirely human. That's part of his character too. Maybe he is caught in late middle age forever. Maybe that is his immortal state. It was a nice touch, anyway, for Rubens to leave his beard in its full brown color but to show the gray peeking out from behind the leaves of Silenus's worldly wreath as he trudges along.

He does trudge, heavy as the earth. Massive haunches and big knees. Just look at the knees of Silenus! Big knotty things connecting two trunks of leg. His calves are big and meaty and straining under his uncertain gait. But the knees, with all their strange little bones and tendons and ligaments. Knees are difficult to understand and almost impossible to love. Rubens pays a lot of attention to the knees of Silenus. He wants to show us all of the parts of the knee, all the sinewy chaos that must be going on underneath the skin during this drunken forward lurching. Maybe that is one measure of Rubens's achievement over and above Titian. Could Titian ever give us the knees of Silenus? Titian was a fine painter, no doubt, but never in a million years could Titian have painted the knees of Silenus. It never would have occurred to him.

* * *

Rubens took Silenus seriously and he took the circumstances that Silenus would have found himself in seriously. If you want proof that Rubens understood the satyr plays then you should go look at his painting of the two satyrs. The painting is at the *Alte Pinakothek* in Munich, Bavaria. That is the same museum where can be found, today, Rubens's painting of the drunken Silenus. The two satyrs painting was painted in 1618 or maybe 1619. It portrays just that, two satyrs, one sipping from a bowl in the background, the other staring straight at us and holding a bunch of grapes in his right hand.

The satyr in the back is no great threat. He's a bit of comic relief. Sipping and spilling his wine, his only purpose in the painting is balance and light and other such matters. It is the lead satyr you can never forget. He looks right in your eyes with that devious smile. "I know," he is saying, "I know what you really want to be doing." That satyr is glowing at the right center of the painting with what he thinks he knows. Maybe he is right. Maybe he has us there. If you want to know what it would look like for a humanoid-type creature to have horns, by the way, here it is in the two satyrs painting. That is the seriousness of Rubens. He has done his morphological homework. He's studied a bunch of goats and other medium-sized horned beasts and then done the painterly labor of working those horns, plausibly, onto a human-shaped skull. You've got to shudder when you notice those satyr horns. Had Rubens been to the forest, seen things there?

Rubens painted the satyrs because he knew what was going on in those satyr plays. He knew what was going on in the places where Silenus spent his time. He understood what was at stake. This is about the earth and the dirt and the crying out in some guttural noise that comes from parts of your body you don't even control. This is about the wild eyes of the drunken man, lurching up in his pointless determination to stumble home. This is about desires that remain ever nameless for the reason that they haven't shape enough to be named. This is the very core of desire, which can never know itself.

Rubens didn't paint those two satyrs because he was brushing up on his mythology or putting the final touches on his mastery of goat morphology. Rubens was painting the sheer animal drive in the eyes of that satyr, and in painting that sheer animal drive he was also painting the intelligence of the satyr, the awareness, the sheepish smile there in the face of the goat/man, the naughty smile that knows about the sheer animal drives and is ashamed and is not ashamed. There's a horror of existence in that leering smile. There is acceptance in it too. Existence is just and only this, the satyr seems to be saying with his devilish grin. I will be this thing. I will be this thing and then I will die.

When Nietzsche tells the Silenus story in his great and awful book he has it that Silenus feels bad for King Midas. King Midas with his eager face, looking forward to the wisdom of Silenus. The way Nietzsche imagines it, Silenus practically begs Midas not to make him speak.

Why do you want to know it? Silenus asks. Why would you want to know the horrible truth about the best thing for man? Why do you force me to tell you that the best thing for man is never to have been born at all?

Silenus doesn't want to tell him, that's the sliver of humanity in the lumbering wreck of Silenus. That's the way Nietzsche imagines Silenus to be speaking to King Midas in the story, and that's the Silenus Rubens painted every time he painted Silenus. He doesn't want to tell anyone the truth because the truth is desolation. He would prefer to remain drunk and mute. What is the point of talking anyway? The greatest wisdom is an unthinkable truth the likes of which no man could really bear. No man could bear that kind of utter and infinite abyss, no matter how powerful, how sinuous his knees, no matter the girth of his trunk, the strength of him.

* * *

There is another painting by Rubens. It is at the small museum on Lange Gasthuisstraat. You can get there by following the route of the number 7 tram going from the National Bank toward the old city in Antwerp. The road turns sharply in an elbow to the right before you get to the museum.

The museum is called the Mayer van den Bergh Museum because that was the name of the rich person who collected all the art. His name was Fritz Mayer van den Bergh though I am told that it was Mayer's mother who really put the museum together after the death of Fritz. She bought a building near the center of Antwerp, not so far from the secret palazzo that Rubens built, and she faked it into something that looks a lot like a sixteenth-century townhouse. That is mildly amusing since Rubens faked his townhouse, too. But Rubens faked his to be a secret Venetian palazzo. Mrs. Van den Bergh built an early twentieth-century house and then faked it to look like something from the sixteenth century. These are the things that people do in Antwerp.

There aren't very many Rubens paintings in the Mayer van den Bergh Museum. There might even be just the one. There aren't very many Rubens paintings in all of Antwerp. Rubens was too big to stay in Antwerp. His paintings got bought off and carried all over the world. But there are a few paintings to be found. A few of the huge biblical scenes are at the Royal Museum in Antwerp. There's a self-portrait hanging at Rubens's house, the secret palazzo. There are a few other paintings scattered around in the smaller museums of Antwerp. And there is a satyr painting at the Mayer van den Bergh Museum. It is on the first floor, in the first room off to your right. The room is set up like a salon, with paintings hung all over the walls. And there it is, the satyr staring straight at us. The second figure in this painting is a woman. She is staring at the satyr on the left-hand side of the painting. His is the same face as the staring satyr from the two satyrs painting in Munich. The same leering smile. The same challenge. The same uncanny horns fused onto the human-shaped skull.

This painting at the Mayer van den Bergh Museum is in a room with terrible lighting. The terrible lighting has the unintentional effect, however, of highlighting exactly how luminous the painting is. It is downright glossy. The first time I walked into that room in the little museum made by Fritz's mother I almost thought that the painting was wet. That is how much it shimmers and shines.

It is said by the people who study these things, that there was a revolution in linseed oil around the time Rubens was painting. That's to say, some of the things Rubens was able to do in applying oil to canvas had to do with a better quality of linseed oil. They used the windmills, the famous windmills of Flanders, to crush up the seeds to make the linseed oil. I never think of those windmills as actually doing anything. I think of them as just being, just waiting and standing out there in the fields. But, in fact, the windmills were churning away in the seventeenth century and one of the things they churned was the seeds of lin that make up linseed oil.

What exactly did Rubens do with the linseed oil? No one is sure, exactly. Painters, it turns out, were exceptionally secretive about the exact materials and procedures they used in those days. It comes, one can imagine, from the idea of the trade and the secrets of the trade that had been handed down since the guilds. It is a medieval mentality. It is a medieval way of thinking. You don't let out the trade secrets. You have secret societies and you have clubhouses and you have oaths and it becomes almost a sacred duty to keep these matters within the club. This is a form of power and it is held tight. Everyone does this, everyone with a craft has this mentality to some degree or another. But within the medieval trades this was practically a way of being, a way of approaching everything in the world.

Anyway, you will hear plenty of painters today, and scholars of the techniques of painting through the ages, complain that they have no idea how Rubens got his translucent glow by which we feel ourselves so taken. We don't know because he didn't want us to know. That's part of the story, surely. Maybe one of the reasons that Rubens was so easily able to understand the secretness of the ancient rites, the hidden things going on amongst the Dionysian cults, was that he himself had experience in the matter. Rubens was part of a secret cult in his own way. He was part of the closed and extremely suspicious society of painters who, emerging from the trade traditions of the Middle Ages, saw it as their own sacred duty to keep the techniques hidden, to reveal the magic of the painting process only through the paintings themselves.

Rubens knew some tricks with linseed oil. He mixed his linseed oil straight from the windmills of Flanders with, more than likely, some other compounds and chemicals that kept it from getting too gloopy or too tacky. I'm not an expert when it comes to the techniques of oil painting. I don't have any specific knowledge about the chemistry. The results, though, are easy to see. In that room at the Mayer van den Bergh Museum, for instance, are plenty of other paintings from the early seventeenth century. Some of these paintings were produced by talented painters. There are a number of paintings of children that hold a particular fascination. But none of these paintings have the luminosity that Rubens's painting of the satyr and the woman achieves. Luminosity isn't even the right word. Rubens manages to make it seem as if light is actually coming from inside the painting out into the room. So maybe luminous is the right word. It is as if the painting itself is shining. The people at the Mayer van den Bergh Museum have actually shone a spotlight on the painting. So, there is quite a lot of light there. But I always have the feeling that the painting would shine like that even if they turned all the lights off. Even if the room were dark, the painting would be making its own light and projecting that light out into the room. What if someone turned off all the lights at the Mayer van den Bergh Museum? What would happen? Would the satyr still be visible, glowing in his own inner light even with complete darkness in the room?

The unworldly shining of that painting corresponds rather well to the lurid smile of the satyr. The satyr knows what is going on in the deep forest glades where his fellow beasts and revelers gather. He knows the secret of those Dionysian ceremonies. And he looks at us with a knowing and infernal smile. He thinks he knows what we really are, at root, too. He knows something about us that he thinks he could show us in a satyr play. He knows that we want to be in the play and so he smiles at us. And Rubens was the one who painted that smile, knew it was a compelling thing to paint. Rubens knew how to paint the smile of the satyr because of the secrets he'd heard about and learned about regarding linseed oil.

6. Is God a goat? What could that possibly mean?

S
O, WHEN RUBENS TOOK TO PAINTING Silenus he wasn't grabbing randomly at the bits of ancient mythology floating around in the intellectual breeze. Rubens had a whole program of satyrs and Dionysus and Silenus. He was bringing the whole story out. He was drawing out an entire tale that comes from the Dionysian rites and the orgies in the forest and the satyr plays that are the very basis for what later became the venerable art of Greek tragedy. Rubens was being very Nietzschean here, if we can be anachronistic—literally anachronistic since it was, in fact, Rubens who came first and Rubens who first painted Silenus as a central figure within this story of Dionysius.

In the preface to his book on tragedy, written much later when Nietzsche was far further along on his path to complete dissolution, Nietzsche asks a funny question: "Is there perhaps (a question for doctors who treat madness) a neurosis associated with health . . . and with youthfulness? What is revealed in that synthesis of god and goat in the satyr?"

Is God a goat? What could that possibly mean?

It is the second question that really startles us, though it is set off by the first. What is revealed by the synthesis of the god and the goat? The union of the god and goat is supposed to reveal something. When I look at those satyr paintings by Rubens and when I look at the satyrs who are constantly hovering around Silenus in the other paintings of Rubens it occurs to me that Rubens would have put the question in much the same way. What is revealed in the synthesis of god and goat in the satyr? And moreover what is it about Silenus that so closely links him to the satyr? Is Silenus the voice of the satyrs? Is he the leader of the satyrs? Is he the prisoner of the satyrs?

What if God were a goat? Would it tell us something about life, what it really is?

The way Nietzsche tells it, when Silenus finally reveals to King Midas the greatest thing for man, that it is best for a man never to have been born and second best for a man to die quickly, Silenus lets out a shrill laugh. Silenus laughs because in telling King Midas the best thing, he actually tells him the worst thing. He tells King Midas what he doesn't want to hear just when the King thought he was going to hear the most wonderful thing. There is cruel laughter in that.

"O suffering creature," Silenus says to King Midas, at least in the way that Nietzsche relates the story.

"O wretched creature born for a day. O child of labor and accident."

"You are forcing me," says Silenus, "to tell you the one thing that you would most like not to hear."

Silenus laughs, knowing that King Midas is going to have his expectations completely upended. King Midas assumes that the best thing for man will, in itself, be a good thing. He is not ready to comprehend the idea that the best thing could be terrible. He hasn't allowed himself, King Midas, fully to contemplate the possibility that man is a wretched creature. He hasn't allowed himself to contemplate the idea that there is no way to apply the value "good" to the process of living a life. But if that is true, if life cannot be described as good, then maybe it shouldn't exist, maybe there is virtue in ending the condition. So that is what Silenus tells King Midas, as Nietzsche relates the story. He reveals to King Midas the deepest possible pessimism.

The Greeks, Nietzsche thinks, the ancient Greeks—the Greeks of the satyr plays and the music in the forest, the Greeks who came before the classical period of Plato and the brilliant days of Greek rationalism, the Greeks before that, the ones who danced the Sicinnis dance and celebrated their secret rites—those Greeks were bold enough to make a health of their pessimism. They were strong, thought Nietzsche, tremendous in their ability to think that pessimism all the way through. Nay, to live that pessimism all the way through. That's the way Nietzsche thought about it.

He had the thought, Nietzsche did, that the madness of the Greeks in their satyr plays and in their Dionysian rites was not the madness of sickness but the madness of health. Is there a madness of health? he wanted to know. Nietzsche asks that in the preface to

Is God a goat? What could that possibly mean?

his book. Is there a madness of health, of youth and of strength? It is a rhetorical question, of course. Nietzsche knows what he thinks. There is indeed a madness of health. There is a mania of health and of youthfulness, the youth of a people, as Nietzsche puts it.

The olden Greeks, the ancient Greeks, thinks Nietzsche understood life under the principle of the goat, the young goat kicking and bucking in the woods. Being connected to the force of life in its most genuine aspect is a matter of goatliness, then. So, even to ask the question of what is good or bad for a man is to lose touch with the primary intuition that God is a goat. That's to say, God is not transcendent, imperturbable, untouchable, unknowable. God is none of those things. God, if God is the God of the world, has to have the characteristics of the goat, the randiness and unpredictability, even the stupidity of the goat.

God is goat because God is truth and the real truth is that life is a matter of running and jumping in the forest and rushing after something to screw and something to eat and, according to Nietzsche in what he thought he learned from the ancient Greeks, even the life of the mind, the intellectual life of the sad-thinking-creature known as man, this creature who must think and make art and make culture, insofar as man does those things, ought to be done with the pure life-expressing power of the goat. Everything else, though Nietzsche, is a lie. Everything other than goats is a lie. There's just no getting around goats, not for the creatures in the forest, not for us, not for the man-goats and satyrs, and not for God.

And so, the question of good and bad for man is canceled before it can be asked. It is preempted. The satyr would never think to ask that question. When King Midas asks the question of Silenus, the first response is silence. It is not a question that a goat would ask. Goats don't ask questions like "what is the best thing for goats?" Goats just go out and express goatliness.

The question about what is best for man is thus equally absurd, since there is nothing special about human beings other than that they think too much and forget that they are more or less hairless goats. What is best for man? How can you even think it? How could King Midas ask the question without embarrassment? How absurd must your premises be for that question to present itself to the mind? All of your presumptions would have to be skewed, utterly out of whack, for you to think that a question like that can be asked, Silenus thinks. Silenus remains silent because there is no way to answer the question. The premises are wrong. There is no answer to it. He is confused, even, by the fact that King Midas is so insistent, that he anticipates a satisfying answer to the question, "What is best for man?"

But King Midas pushes Silenus. He must know. He will not allow Silenus to leave until the question has been answered. Silenus is still struggling with a question to which there can be no answer since the very phrasing of it has gotten everything wrong, has made assumptions about life at its root that are profoundly mistaken. Then

Is God a goat? What could that possibly mean?

Silenus laughs, to himself and finally at King Midas. He has figured out an answer. His answer will be the demolition of the very question. He will answer in such a way that the answer destroys the premises that could have led to such a misguided question.

"The best thing for man?" Silenus repeats, laughing.

"If you want to think that we can apply standards like good and bad to it, to this force of such tremendous upwelling that the question is utterly absurd, but if you want to ask the absurd, then the answer is that the best thing for a man is not to have been born at all."

"Oh, you have been born? The unfortunate has already occurred? Well, in that case there is only one thing to be done, you who seek what is best for man. The only way to remedy the situation, since you are so concerned with what is good and what is bad, is to die. And for goodness' sake, do it quickly. Get yourself dead."

And thus the question falls apart. It has been destroyed. And Silenus is released back into the forest.

7. Older Nietzsche upbraids Younger Nietzsche for not being crazy enough. That's to say, Nietzsche goes all in on being Nietzsche and then goes to war.

A LITTLE LESS THAN FIFTEEN YEARS after he wrote *The Birth of Tragedy*, Nietzsche wrote a preface to the book. The preface was his chance to look back at the book that made him Nietzsche, as it were—that is, the book that turned him into the Nietzsche that we all know as Nietzsche today.

The Older Nietzsche reads through *The Birth of Tragedy* and finds some of the things that Younger Nietzsche wrote a little bit funny, worth poking some fun at. That's the feeling one gets from reading Nietzsche's preface, written in 1886, to *The Birth of Tragedy*, which was published in 1872. He's had some time to think, Nietzsche has, and he has had some time to become even more crazy than he was in the early 1870s and to feel some disgust for the younger man who wrote *The Birth of Tragedy*, and some annoyance that the younger version of himself hadn't been even more wild, more honest, more personal and more relentless in writing that book.

Nietzsche even goes so far as to suggest, in his later preface, that he should just have written *The Birth of Tragedy* as a kind of Dionysian poem! Thank God, we can all sigh with relief, that he did not, since, among many things that Nietzsche was not very good at was writing poetry and, also, to his eternal frustration, writing music. Older Nietzsche thinks that he should have written *The Birth of Tragedy* as a wild bit of Dionysian opera that would have topped everything Wagner had ever written—Wagner, the man whose musical genius tortured Nietzsche to the very end.

Of course, Nietzsche was wrong about that since he was a terrible poet and an awful composer, although he was, undeniably good at the very thing he did in *The Birth of Tragedy*, which was to write a piece of lyrical prose that, whatever its faults and problems, which are many, is utterly and completely unforgettable and which, for the person who reads it truly, reads it with genuine understanding and with the willingness to let its ideas penetrate into the soul, as it were, is never going to be the same. To read *The Birth of Tragedy* and to understand in one's soul what is being said is to be shaken to one's core, as they say, and to come out the other side a transformed person, for better or worse. What a person does with the soul-shaking experience of reading *The Birth of Tragedy* is that person's own business. That's up to you. Perhaps the only truly honest thing is to go and die. That's an option. Or to truly live for a few moments and then to die. Or to fall apart. Or to finally and for once put oneself together. Or to run away. Or to come back again for the first time.

But for Nietzsche, the experience of looking back at his first book was the feeling of admiration at his own greatness and then simultaneous frustration with himself for not being greater still. In this, Nietzsche is like the rest of us, only more so. He looks back at himself and looking back at the young Nietzsche who was obsessed with Silenus he can't help making a little bit of fun of the youthful version of himself, so eager to spill his ideas out upon the world. But he admires himself for it, too. Older Nietzsche is amazed with Younger Nietzsche, so on fire to bring the wisdom of Silenus back into the world again after so long an absence.

"How did I do it?" Nietzsche wonders about himself in writing a preface, many years later, to the little book that thrust the wisdom of Silenus back into a world, which, Older Nietzsche realizes, never much wanted it in the first place, has never wanted it since then, and will never really want it. That's what Older Nietzsche laughs at himself for in his preface: he laughs at Younger Nietzsche for thinking that the world was going to change, that the world was at the cusp of some kind of deep and inevitable renewal. That, Older Nietzsche realizes, was never going to happen. The younger versions of ourselves always think that the world is on the cusp of some tremendous transformation and the older versions of ourselves always realize that this was wrong. Nietzsche had that same realization and moreover, had a book in his hands that manifested the foolish hopes of a younger version of himself. He could hold the book in his hands and commune, as it were, with the person who once thought that his little book was a harbinger of a new age. Older Nietzsche could hold the book of the Younger Nietzsche and laugh.

But he can't laugh it all away. He can't laugh it all away because he also feels that Younger Nietzsche was right about the truth of Silenus being the truth of life lived in its utmost honesty. That's why Older Nietzsche can't let *The Birth of Tragedy* go, not completely. That's also why Older Nietzsche's preface to the book of Younger Nietzsche is titled, amusingly, "An Attempt at Self-Criticism." Not actual self-criticism, mind you, but an "attempt" at it. In the end, he can't bring himself to genuine self-criticism for the simple reason that he is Nietzsche, and Nietzsche's mind and prose only ever worked in the mode of fundamental self-assurance. Being self-assured and being self-critical don't really go together, except in the sense, which Nietzsche manifests in his preface, that one criticizes an earlier version of oneself for not having been, at the time, self-assured enough. That's basically what Nietzsche does in his preface.

He says, in essence, "You, Younger Nietzsche, ought to have been even more self-assured, more willing to tell your truth without hesitation, and more realistic about the fact that your undeniable truths were going to fall onto the deaf ears of a humanity that never has been and never will be prepared to hear the truth, full-throttle, from the mouth of a genuine prophet."

It is an amazing thing for Older Nietzsche to say to Younger Nietzsche since not many people over the last hundred and fifty years have objected that *The Birth of Tragedy* is too timid a book. But that's what Older Nietzsche thought.

So Older Nietzsche wonders, in his preface, why he, alone among men, had the strength and fortitude and genius to see that Silenus is still relevant, that Silenus still has the last word on life. Nietzsche does not say right out that he is the only one with genius enough to face Silenus but that is essentially what he is saying.

It is clear that Nietzsche nominates himself as the great heir to the wisdom of Silenus, the great genius of Silenusian life. He realizes, in writing his preface to the book many years later, that there was something personal, something "deeply personal," in writing the original book, *The Birth of Tragedy*, and that the deeply personal feelings were tied up with the historical moment in which he was writing. History was happening outside, while Nietzsche was inside, living in the Alps and thinking thoughts about Silenus. And what must be understood here is that Nietzsche, when he started writing *The Birth of Tragedy*, thought he was writing an untimely book that none of his contemporaries would understand and that would isolate him even further in the world. Nietzsche was running away from life, running away from his academic job, running to his hideout in the Alps (Germans always run away to the

Alps when they feel misunderstood) and writing a book that would be his own personal rejection and denouncement of his own time, his condemnation of his own historical period as a period of cowardice and a general unwillingness to face the hard truth of Silenus.

But as Nietzsche scribbled away in the Alps, the Franco-Prussian War was raging outside, not so far away, and Nietzsche, reflecting on this little war as he was writing, began to see himself as both removed from and yet deeply connected to the events transpiring outside. The Franco-Prussian War was disturbing to Younger Nietzsche. That's how Older Nietzsche describes it. He was disturbed and living in what he calls a "disturbing era." He seems to think, Nietzsche does, that writing this book in his corner of the Alps while momentous events occur outside in the world is both the context for the book, the thing which explains the fact of his book coming to be, and also that his book is being written "in spite of" these events.

What he means, really, is that his very book is the true Franco-Prussian War, that his book about Silenus is the spiritual truth underlying the events of the Franco-Prussian War and that, in the end, the Franco-Prussian War was not up to the task of fulfilling in the world the pronouncements of his brilliant little book.

The Franco-Prussian War made Younger Nietzsche realize how important his little book about tragedy really was. Younger Nietzsche, scribbling away in the Alps, begins to suspect that his book isn't so untimely after all. Maybe, he thinks, the Germans are ready to wake up, to give the decadent and soulless French the military thrashing they deserve, and to grasp once again the madness of youthfulness and health.

"Here I am writing this devastating little book and the Franco-Prussian War comes along to finish the job for me," Nietzsche starts to think, mulling it over in his Alpine hideaway, "and maybe history is on my side and this little war will remake the world in earnest and release the truth of Silenus after the long years of slumbering."

Nietzsche lets himself get excited, runs down from his Alpine redoubt, and decides to be present "on the battlefield," as he puts it, for this great historical moment when the German people will finally wake up and grab hold of their destiny.

But what happened instead, over the years from the time Younger Nietzsche wrote the *Birth of Tragedy* to the time Older Nietzsche wrote his later preface, is that the German people proved themselves, at least according to Older Nietzsche, to be less than ready for greatness and for releasing the Dionysian mob and the truth of Silenus.

The Franco Prussian War, in essence, as Nietzsche saw it, let him down. The war was not up to the task of remaking the world, which Younger Nietzsche was, indirectly, demanding that the world do, demanding with his book that the world be remade by the long forgotten truth of Silenus. That's why he wrote the book, Nietzsche came to realize, sitting in his hideout up in the Alps. I am writing this little book to blow a hole right through the middle of the world, thought Younger Nietzsche.

Up in the Alps, he was wracked with tensions and conflicting emotions, was Younger Nietzsche. He didn't know whether to ignore the stupid world, which would never wake up, or to jump back into the fray with hopes for a new age. He was feeling especially reflective and perplexed. He was extremely distressed and yet also completely carefree, as he later described those Alpine days. And as he wrote his book, the thunderclap of the Battle of Wörth was resounding across Europe. This is what Nietzsche calls it, a thunderclap. Why is it a thunderclap? Presumably, it is a thunderclap because it was at the Battle of Wörth that a collection of German armies of the not-yet declared German Empire handed a resounding defeat to the French armies. We say that, a resounding defeat. That is what Nietzsche means by the thunderclap. It resounded. Everyone could hear it. What did it mean? It meant that a new German Empire was coming to be just as Nietzsche was writing his little book that was supposed to be about long-dead, long-ancient Greek things that have only a wispy relation to the here and now.

"But wait a second, holy shit!" Younger Nietzsche realizes sitting in his isolated room in the Alps writing a book that, by all rights, no one in the world should give a damn about.

"Doesn't his book amount to the greatest wake-up call of all time?" Younger Nietzsche thinks to himself, "and aren't we, the German people, finally waking up to our historical destiny and finally giving the French the tremendous thrashing that they have for so long deserved, and will not the forthcoming coup de grace, which, it so turns out, comes in the form of the Battle of Wörth, will not this culminating blow to the French and, by extension, to all the lies and the perfidies of modern life, will not this thunderclap," is how Nietzsche puts it, "this thunderclap of a battle wake up an entire nation to its historical destiny?"

That's what Younger Nietzsche thinks to himself and he thinks it so hard that he jumps up from his little room in the Alps and runs down to be there, to be present at the historical moment when the German people will wake to the call of Silenus and to the wild music of Dionysus. The Franco-Prussian War is not just a little European War, thinks young Nietzsche. No, in fact it is the moment at which the ancient forces of Real Life will stir and make themselves known through the indomitable power and force of the German people. But of course Younger Nietzsche was completely wrong about all of this, Older Nietzsche realized. As correct as he may have been about the essential truths of life, he had been perhaps, Older Nietzsche confesses in his preface, somewhat hasty, a tad optimistic in his hopes for the Franco-Prussian War as a transformation of the entire world.

Why do we care about any of this? How many people, today, even realize that there was a Franco-Prussian War in 1870? How many people have ever heard it mentioned that there was a Battle of Wörth and that this battle resounded at all, let alone like a thunderclap? If there was a thunderclap in 1870, that thunderclap was silenced long, long ago.

Except that, maybe not. Maybe not. Maybe that thunderclap, the thunderclap of a strange and forgotten and obscure war in the late nineteenth century, still resounding, as it were, maybe that thunderclap is still ringing in our heads even though we don't know the origins of the thunder. Maybe it is all just one fucking war, a war that has never stopped but that is all just the same one, now here, now there, but the same war repeating itself over and over again like echoes that keep bouncing infinitely back and forth across a valley flanked by giant mountains. Maybe the thunder never dies completely and is always renewed by fresh claps, as it were, fresh outbreaks of the giant noise that is the One Infinite Ongoing War.

The specific thunderclap of the Battle of Wörth led to a series of momentous events that Nietzsche, soon to completely lose his mind and then to die, would never witness and which would find the Germans and the French sitting around a table at Versailles signing documents twice more. The Franco-Prussian War is, essentially, World War I in its first manifestation and World War I is, of course, also World War II and World War II, you could say, hasn't ever really stopped either, and none of this could have started without the Franco-Prussian War since, if you'd like to be audacious about it, you could trace a line from the Battle of Troy all the way to the Battle of Wörth—which, if you allow yourself to think about it for a moment, raises the fascinating and terrifying thought that we have never even finished fighting the Battle of Troy.

Nietzsche, of course, could never have known about World War I or the Cold War, or the exact course that this drama was going to take after the thunderclap at Wörth, but he had his intuitions. He describes himself as being in a state of the deepest tensions during that period.

Nietzsche describes himself as being "under the walls of Metz" (and one presumes he means this both literally and metaphorically), while his book about tragedy is still stewing in his mind. Nietzsche had gone to Metz because he wanted to be present for a transformation in history. He left his mountain redoubt and traveled to the very gates of Metz. He wanted to be present for the defeat of France and to see the awakening of the German people. He cannot finish his book. His mind is still in ferment and doubt because he isn't quite sure whether his book is heralding a new age or not. Will it really happen? Will the Franco-Prussian War let loose the Dionysian horde? Nietzsche was still there at Metz, or nearby, when Napoleon III finally surrendered and became, this emperor of France, a prisoner more or less, to the forces of the nascent German Empire.

"Thank God," thinks Younger Nietzsche, "thank God that the sniveling French have actually been truly and decisively defeated, and with the defeat of the sniveling French the defeat of that form of French rationalism, that form of French Enlightenment that would smother the truth of Dionysus with the lies of so-called Reason, which are the lies of Socrates that have deluded us for so long into thinking that we can make sense of this life, and order it and control it, instead of simply letting it bubble and flow through us."

The thought is, in fact, entirely insane in the very literal sense of the word, but it is clear that Younger Nietzsche sitting under the gates of Metz and reveling in the defeat of the whimpering French is actually gloating in what he considers a great defeat of that old dog Socrates by Silenus and Dionysus. Napoleon III is not really Napoleon III, thinks Nietzsche, he's Socrates, my old enemy Socrates dressed up in French finery.

The French are only a minor distraction here, Nietzsche realizes as he scampers down from his mountain redoubt to glory in the birth of a new and wilder Germany. The French are not really the French, they are the armies of Socrates, they are the armies of Apollo, they are the armed manifestation of the life's deepest lies. Socrates and Apollo and the French and Jesus, who we might as well throw in there too, are all in league with the central lie, which is the lie that life can be made better, or that it has a purpose, or that it can be approached through the lens of morality, which is the central lie that life is better one way rather than another, when, in truth, the truth of Silenus, there is simply life expressing itself in the glorious pointlessness of pure expression and then passing away, and there is no code and no direction and no plan and nothing but a furious unfolding, and one can either unfold furiously along with it, or one can live a lie, like those great tricksters Socrates and Christ, though in the end even living a lie doesn't matter because, for all the brilliant lying of Socrates and Christ Jesus and the French, it's all going to get blown away in the furious unfolding anyway. And as Younger Nietzsche stands under the gates of Metz, his little Dionysian book festering in his gloriously addled brain, he becomes convinced, if only for a short while (a conviction, by the way, that Older, even crazier Nietzsche will rue), he becomes convinced, does Younger Nietzsche, that the historical tide is turning and that the great and pitiless German people are going to rise up and sweep across the lands with a new Dionysian truth.

Only after being present for the culmination of the Franco-Prussian War was Nietzsche able to calm down, get back up to the Alps, and finish his book. He had a bit of a cold, maybe a mild flu. But he says in the preface that he contracted that illness "in the field." Those are the words he used, "in the field," which is to say that even Older Nietzsche maintained the fantasy that he was down around Metz as, essentially, a soldier in the German army. The actual soldiers in the army surely did not consider Nietzsche a combatant, but he seems to have seen himself as such, and not just as any combatant. He saw himself as the greatest combatant of them all, sickly Nietzsche there on the battlefield with his little book, wielding it like a weapon against the French and all the forces of historical cowardice. Nietzsche, in Nietzsche's own mind, was, in short, the one and true hero of the Franco-Prussian War. But in the end no one listened to him, the German people refused to wake up, and he was forced to write several more increasingly bitter versions of *The Birth of Tragedy* until he became finally and irreversibly insane.

All these matters got more and more mixed up in Nietzsche's mind: A nation and a book, a people and an idea, a god and a goat and a drunken old man who follows behind on a donkey.

8. All of history is connected and it is connected primarily through war. And then, hidden within this history, is another story, a story of peace, which is for broken people and losers. Also, you don't fuck with William the Silent.

THE FRANCO-PRUSSIAN WAR WAS Nietzsche's own personal war. But really there is just one war and it has been going on forever. You can ride the echo back from the shots being fired on the Mesopotamian planes of Iraq and Syria right now at the writing of this sentence and you can trace those shots back through the Cold War and back to World War II and to Hitler in the train car in the forest, forcing the French to sign a treaty in revenge for World War I and you can follow the echo back further, bringing Prussia back into being, sending Nietzsche again back under the walls of Metz, unwinding the Napoleonic Wars and arriving back again at the first Battle of Wörth in which the French Revolutionary forces were handing a series of military defeats to the forces of the *ancien régime*.

You could go back further than that. You could go back before the French Revolution to when the Bourbon kings were sitting at their thrones and planning battles here and there in their constant warring with the House of Hapsburg. And what are the Hapsburgs, really, but the forces left over from the Holy Roman Empire? So it goes back. Every bit of intrigue and war and killing takes you back to previous intrigues and to previous arrangements of power and might and to the intrigues and killing of a previous era. You can roll the historical trajectory back and forth all you like, zooming in on one period of the great and everlasting war or onto another period of that endless and exhausting and never-to-be-concluded war.

Rolling back the story from the early eighteenth century into the seventeenth century we land ourselves smack into the middle of a particularly nasty period of mayhem and murder known, rather antiseptically, as the Thirty Years' War, which had broken out across the extremely disorganized and non-unified lands of what would later be called the nation of Germany. But it wasn't Germany yet. That would only come with Nietzsche and the walls of Metz. The lands were disorganized and under the control of various German princes and ruling families. German, but not yet Germany. And in Flanders—at the center of which is Antwerp—for persons living at the time of the conflicts between the Bourbons and the Holy Roman Hapsburgs you had to be very careful how you chose and managed your allegiances.

What I'm saying is that Rubens, just like Nietzsche, was living in a confusing and unsettling time. But are there any other kinds of times? The wars that raged and were about to rage around Antwerp were percolating in Rubens's mind just as the Franco-Prussian War was percolating in Nietzsche's mind.

* * *

The father of Peter Paul Rubens, Jan Rubens, was a public figure in Flanders at the time of the conflicts between the Bourbons and the Holy Roman Hapsburgs, a conflict that had heated up with the religious battles between those who wanted to follow Rome and those who didn't. This matter of religion was, itself, causing many complicated tensions within the territories otherwise understood to be roughly within the sphere of influence of the Holy Roman Hapsburgs.

Jan Rubens, a lawyer, an attorney of sorts and reasonably ambitious (we are led to believe) figure in the politics of Flanders at the time, was involved at the local level, if we can call it that, with the various questions that beset Flanders in those days, Flanders being within the sphere of influence of the Holy Roman Hapsburgs and, simultaneously, influenced by the ideas of religious reform coming directly from the areas to the North, the Dutch areas, and from the parts of Northern Germany that were just to the East.

We are talking about Protestants here, obviously, and of Papists. The Pope, as we know, is a Catholic.

Flanders found itself as a small Holy Roman Hapsburg zone pinched between the Bourbon power to its south and the anti-Hapsburg powers to the North and to the North East, between Protestants and Papists, between warring powers, in a very, very tight spot.

So, for an individual living in Flanders at that time, the time that the Rubens family was trying to make its way in the world, for a family getting along in Flanders at that time there were questions of politics, questions of geo-politics and the longstanding tensions between the Bourbons and the Holy Roman Hapsburgs, and there were also questions of a religious nature, personal questions as to how you worshiped God and how you viewed the church, which themselves mapped onto political and geographical concerns, though not always in the most straightforward way. Complicated.

When you lived in Flanders at the time the Rubens family lived in Flanders, you had to play a tricky game of allegiances and you had to know how to split the difference, as it were, you had to know how to play the game. You had to know who you were talking to at any given moment and you had to be ready to switch it up on a dime when talking to the next person you might bump into on any given day. Getting it wrong could have serious consequences, like, for instance, having your skin ripped off and then being cut into small pieces and having those pieces scattered namelessly in a field. Or being gutted like an animal out in the street. Different kinds of consequences.

It has sometimes been claimed, by people who dig into history and make such claims, that Jan Rubens was an Anabaptist. Anabaptists were Protestants. But Anabaptists were Protestants with a vengeance, Protestants taking the basic ideas of Luther and running way past what the old master ever intended. Anabaptists went way out on a limb, taking some of the stuff Jesus says in the Gospels so seriously that they were, in essence, no longer trustworthy as citizens of any state. If you take some of what Jesus says very seriously, take him at his word, as it were, then you can't give your allegiance to any worldly power now can you? How could you? Jesus, in this sense, was always a radical and the Anabaptists were willing to go right along with the most radical implications of what Jesus had to say, for instance, in his Sermon on the Mount.

I'm not going to take the time proving this to you. Just grab a Bible and read the Sermon on the Mount and then ask yourself how it would be possible to actually live according to the basic ideas Jesus dumps on us there and not be a total and complete radical, utterly opposed in every way to the regulations and rules of any society on earth, which definitely includes Flanders in the sixteenth century.

No, to be an Anabaptist was to read the things Jesus said and did and then, for some reason, actually go out and try to live exactly in the way he describes, as if Jesus actually meant that life could be lived according to the insanely radical things that came out of his mouth. The Anabaptists went out and did that and this created, in other Christians, a lust for murdering them, which shouldn't be all that surprising, really, given that even Nietzsche, a man little given to the Christian life, once commented to the effect that there has only really been one Christian in world history, one person actually willing to commit to the incredible and uncompromising things entailed by the ideas of the Sermon on the Mount, and that the one honest-to-goodness Christian in world history is the one who died on the Cross.

But the early Anabaptists came pretty close and that's why so many other Christians were so lustfully eager to slaughter them.

Even the other more mainstream Protestants turned their backs on the Anabaptists. Even Lutherans enjoyed killing Anabaptists, that's how far into radicalism the Anabaptists had gone. So, if Jan Rubens became an Anabaptist then he was most assuredly not screwing around. He'd been radicalized, somehow. We don't know what motivated Jan toward Anabaptist ideas nor do we know, truly, whether Jan Rubens ever did proclaim himself an Anabaptist in the strict sense of the term. He may have been of two minds about the matter. He may have wavered. He was, though, accused of being an Anabaptist and this seems to have finally led to the Rubens family fleeing Antwerp altogether, because you just couldn't be an Anabaptist in Antwerp in those days for long without getting yourself murdered, and so the family had to flee Antwerp and take up residence in the city of Siegen, an area that was soon to become devastated by the Thirty Years' War and which, much later, would become part of the territory of the German Empire after the defeat of the French during the Battle of Wörth that so overwhelmed the young Nietzsche. And it was in Siegen, in fact, that Jan Rubens managed to put himself in a situation of such humiliation and disgrace that he was, in fact, never to recover and to live out the remainder of his life, as far as we can tell, as a broken man.

* * *

We'll never know, probably, just how much the young Peter Paul Rubens, our painter, was affected by this story of humiliation and disgrace, how much he was aware of it as the immediate history of his father's life. Rubens's father was, though, in the years just before the birth of Peter Paul Rubens, arrested. And for a time it looked as if he might be put to death.

The whole thing happened because of love. Jan Rubens, the father of our painter Rubens, fell in love with Anna of Saxony. Anna of Saxony was of the House of Wettin, and without going into the detailed and complicated matters of European aristocratic lineage, it can be said that the House of Wettin was an important family within the area of Northern Germany that was both heavily interested in the ideas of Martin Luther and heavily interested politically in alliances that could bring some leverage against the forces and the influences of the Holy Roman Hapsburgs.

You could say, then, that in geopolitical terms and in terms of the nasty business going on with religion and with killing at the end of the sixteenth century in Europe, Jan Rubens had managed to go right to the hottest of spots and to get himself up close and personal with the hottest of people, if we can call them that. Because, for reasons of power and reasons of influence and all the maneuverings of the important families of the time, Anne of Saxony had become a key vector of various family alliances and had found herself married to William of Orange, of all people, who later became known to history as William the Silent.

One of the basic and undeniable truths of the history of the late sixteenth century in Northern Europe is that you don't fuck with William the Silent. Fucking with William the Silent is fucking with one of the most serious and most inscrutable and least perturbable and, well, least fuckwithable figures of the era, and Jan Rubens, the father of our famous painter, went so far as to fuck with William the Silent by means of fucking his wife.

William of Orange can be said to have almost single-handedly started the Eighty Years' War and who cares, really, what the Eighty Years' War was all about? It's just another explosion of killing and outrages and murder in the everlasting and ongoing war. But William of Orange was right there in the heart of all the killing, the religious killing and the political killing and the intrigues that shaped the time, as they say.

It was due to the actions of William of Orange and his brothers, in fact, that the Dutch revolt against the powers of the Holy Roman Hapsburgs in their Spanish incarnation finally turned into full-blown war. This war would later become known to history as the aforementioned Eighty Years' War, which is quite a long war, when you think of it, and it is a war that overlaps, in both time and purpose, with the Thirty Years' War, which would devastate the lands throughout that part of the world that would, many years later, come to be known as Germany. You could even say that the hard-assed maneuvering by which William the Silent initiated the Eighty Years' War, which morphed into the Thirty Years' War, which destroyed the nascent Germany of the time, was the preface through which Prussia finally transformed itself, in Nietzsche's time, into the German Empire, which Nietzsche, for a short time, mistakenly thought was the historical window through which Dionysus and his tutor Silenus were going to step onto the stage of world history once more.

* * *

William of Orange was assassinated in July of 1584 by an agent of the Holy Roman Hapsburgs and so would witness little of the events of the Eighty Years' War that he had done so much to initiate nor of the Thirty Years' War, which he did not directly initiate, being deceased, but can be said to have heavily influenced with his armed revolt against the Holy Roman Hapsburgs before he was finally assassinated by those very same forces. William the Silent was taken so seriously by his foes, in short, that there was a more or less constant plot to assassinate him for much of his life. He was, essentially, being assassinated for twenty years straight until one of those assassinations finally took hold for good. What happened in the end is that a man named Balthasar Gérard stalked William the Silent for years and, when finally getting the chance to sit down with him at dinner one evening, pulled out a pair of pistols and blasted away at close range until William the Silent was, at long last, really and truly silent. Monsieur Gérard, we might mention, was captured by the friends and allies of William the Silent not long after blowing William out of his chair with a pair of flintlock pistols. Gérard was tortured in various heinous and unspeakable ways, hot tongs and the ripping of flesh were involved, and then, among other indignities, had his heart ripped out of his chest and flung into his own face just before being finally, and no doubt mercifully, beheaded. The point is, once again, that the stakes were rather high in dealing with William the Silent and that fucking with William the Silent did not tend to end, for anyone, pleasantly.

Twenty or so years before he was assassinated, though, William the Silent, in 1561, married Anna of Saxony in a sort of power move to consolidate family relationships and all those sorts of things that aristocrats of the time were given to doing. We do not know very much about his personal feelings regarding Anna. We do know that William was rarely at home during his marriage to Anna and that his activities, which would later coalesce into activities of outright revolt against the Holy Roman Hapsburgs, were of a pressing nature. He was pressed.

We also know that Anna of Saxony was William the Silent's second wife. His first wife was Anna van Egmont. They had three children together. And then she died. She was twenty-five years old when she died. It has been said that William's first marriage was a happy one and that the death of Anna van Egmont was difficult for William the Silent, a claim not hard to understand. The second marriage, then, to Anna of Saxony, a marriage made largely, perhaps solely, for reasons of geopolitics, could easily be thought of as a distant marriage, a marriage in which the two parties kept their distance. William the Silent, it could be surmised, was never truly to fall in love again after the death of his first wife. For William the Silent, the years between the death of his first wife and his eventual assassination were years of politics and war. Love was not a factor.

* * *

Anna of Saxony, being of an aristocratic family infused with much wealth, had lands and holdings and interests to negotiate. Like rich people throughout the ages she needed a lawyer. She hired Jan Rubens as her legal advisor. It is not clear, exactly, what a legal advisor to an important royal personage during the late sixteenth century would have been doing all day long. He was helping Anna of Saxony manage her affairs. But whatever else he was doing, he managed to pitch his woo as well, as the saying goes. Or maybe she pitched her woo. We don't know. It is hard to imagine that Jan Rubens was being ambitious or clever in this circumstance. William I of Orange, later to be known to history as William the Silent, the husband of Anne of Saxony, was not, surely, going to be pleased about the situation. And having the displeasure of William I of Orange was not a good thing, as we have already made clear, and as it did not turn out to be for Jan Rubens, who was to spend a number of years in prison awaiting execution for his troubles.

That fact alone makes it plausible that there was, actually, love between Jan Rubens and Anna of Saxony. It makes a scenario plausible in which, as the two worked together looking over the legal matters to which Anna had to attend, there was some kind of force, some kind of attraction that started to draw them together. Jan Rubens started to think about his time with Anna of Saxony more and more often. Anna of Saxony found herself waking up late at night with a strange heaviness in her breast, anticipating the continued labor over her legal matters, yearning for more time spent with him. One can imagine Jan Rubens engaged in laborious and not entirely persuasive conversations with his actual wife, the future mother of our painter Rubens, explaining to her that the legal matters pertaining to Anna of Saxony were becoming more and more pressing, requiring more and more of his time and attention.

Are any of the parties in such affairs ever really completely ignorant as to the situation at hand? Maybe we always know—everyone always knows. And yet the charade must go on, the increasingly futile explanations and the increasingly desperate attempts to convey to everyone that nothing is going on when, in fact, it is patently clear that something is going on. It is all we have, that charade, the various roles to play, the inability to find the specific language and set of actions that would cut through and lay bare the actual state of affairs. Maybe we don't want to cut through it anyway, since all we have are the roles and the charade, roles that are, in a way, an alternative to the abyss.

Whatever the case, the affair between Jan Rubens and Anna of Saxony developed into a serious matter and, eventually, came to the attention of William the Silent, who had them both arrested. They were to be put to the sword, or have their faces ripped off, or have hot oil poured into their bums, or executed in some other way that would have pleased the people of the time, who genuinely, it should be mentioned, seemed to enjoy watching such things.

Finally, they were not. Other things happened. Jan Rubens survived, went back to his wife Maria, and the both of them became the parents of Peter Paul Rubens, who would eventually move back to Antwerp and build his house there, in the ruined city caught between the historical and geographical affairs of the Bourbons and the Holy Roman Hapsburgs and the Dutch in their revolt.

9. Civilization has its limits. We fear those limits. We also seek those limits.

IF YOU ROLL THINGS VERY FAR BACK before these times of conflict between the Bourbons and the Holy Roman Hapsburgs, times that when rolled forward lead directly to the events of the Napoleonic Wars and then to the events of the founding of the German Empire that so inspired and simultaneously disappointed Nietzsche, if you roll back very quickly over centuries and centuries, back past even the times when the stories and legends about Silenus were being told by the ancient Greeks in the time of the discovery and invention of Greek tragedy, you go past that and everything falls away completely. You enter into a black hole of sorts, a place where there is nothing at all.

Many years ago, rolling this specific story back as far as it will go, the civilizations of the eastern Mediterranean were destroyed by The Sea Peoples. These were the Homeric times, not the times in which Homer lived, but the times from which the stories of Homeric heroes emerged. These are the times of

Agamemnon and of Troy. Just saying those names has a kind of mystery and splendor, does it not? We were just speaking of William the Silent and Anne of Saxony and then, with a tiny shift of the historical register, we come to the names Agamemnon and the name of the place called Troy. These are the times of the Mycenaean civilization and the Hittite civilization. Who are The Sea Peoples, you ask? We don't know. The story goes back a long time. It goes back to the Age of Heroes, to the eastern Mediterranean during the Bronze Age.

But sometime during the thirteenth century BCE, bad things started to happen.

There had been a lot of prosperity around Greece and the areas of what is now Turkey in the years leading up to the thirteenth century BCE. The great Mycenaean civilization was working on its greatness. The great Hittite empire over on the Near Eastern side was greater still and working on that. Populations were rising, great cities were being built. Just look at all the treasures that the archeologists keep finding in the shaft graves. The great kings of the eastern Mediterranean. They had riches to bury. They had palaces to build. They had slaves to capture and things to make the slaves do after they'd captured them.

And then the prosperity started to wane. Maybe the population growth was too fast. Maybe a series of natural disasters started the ruination. Maybe there was famine from a few years of bad crops. Probably it was many things. Probably the great war against Troy, about which the blind poet Homer was to sing five hundred years or so later, probably that expedition happened during the beginning of the years of decline, the years when raiding nearby cities seemed like a more and more attractive proposition.

It is true, by the way. It is true that an actual group of actual men on this very earth on which the city, for instance, of Antwerp can, today, be found to exist, on this very same earth over three thousand years ago a group of men did decide to muster their forces and sail out against a real city, Troy. They did it. There was a Trojan War. We'll never know exactly what it was really like. But it was real. When the men came back from Troy, things were not going so well at home. The city-states of Greece were at one another's throats. Things were unraveling according to a sort of inexorable logic, the logic of unraveling. Anyone who has experienced any form of unraveling is aware of the internal logic of the thing. You know the feel of it, if you've been through it, any version of the unraveling. A little unraveling leads to more unraveling and that leads to even more. I believe you can feel when that starts to happen. I believe that the feeling of unraveling becomes seductive in its own terrible way. I believe that many human beings, when they start to feel an unraveling coming on, start to get excited about it even if they are embarrassed about that fact and don't talk about it much with one another. But they are excited by the idea of unraveling even as they are scared of it. Something is drawing them down, some lust for destruction. I believe that a certain glee, a certain almost erotic flavor to the possibility of unraveling and its inherent violence begins to take root in the hearts of women and men. Maybe that feeling is something we know very well. Maybe it is something that the satyr is showing us, the look on his face the way Rubens paints him, desire spiraling downward, just down.

The Greeks, the Mycenaeans of the later days of the Bronze Age, would have known that feeling well. They would have known the fear of it. Is there any fear more real than the fear that takes hold when you feel the reality of the unraveling? I don't think there is. The fear is all the worse for the desire in it. Let there be war, then, you say. Let it all come down. Let the heavens be unleashed. Increase the unraveling.

And then when it really gets going you want to pull back. You want to go home again. You want to feel the warm embrace of home. But you cannot. The unraveling has gone too far. Sometimes I think of Warsaw when I think about that kind of unraveling. I think of the people emerging from the rubble of Warsaw at the end of the Second World War, in the period after Hitler went to that train car to accept the surrender of the French in the same place where the Germans had signed the Treaty of Versailles after their defeat in the First World War. The second half of the Second World War is a period of a great unraveling.

Czeslaw Milosz, the great Polish writer and poet, describes, somewhere in one of his writings, the shock of seeing his first building blown open by a bomb. There it is, the insides are on the outsides. Something irreversible has happened. The private space of the home has been blown out into the public space of the city. It is obscene, frightening. That is when the unraveling has passed the point of no return. The way the people of a city suddenly rise up as one and go out into the streets for killing. They do that when the unraveling is upon them. They do it all the time. Just look at the Warsaw Uprising, which leaves a final result that can only be described as nothing. There is nothing left. The civilization that once existed there has been wiped away, almost to the bone.

They did it in Antwerp during the times of the religious wars, the times that Rubens himself stood there and witnessed. The way people rushed into the churches to burn and destroy. The Reformation was an unraveling. It was unleashing the satyrs, who never know when to stop because it is their very nature to pull the stops out.

The Mycenaeans, in the olden days, the days even before the Greeks had started to develop the cultic practices that would later evolve into the theatrical form known as tragedy, turned on one another. They sent seven captains of the Argive army against Thebes. They brought down their own cities. And at some point during this whole unraveling, The Sea Peoples saw an opportunity. Maybe The Sea Peoples were tribes at the outlying regions of the eastern Mediterranean. Maybe they came from even further away. It is hard to know. The Sea Peoples were agents of destruction, and agents of destruction don't leave much trace. The Mycenaean civilization collapsed completely and the Hittite civilization collapsed completely. They just fell apart, they disintegrated. It is as if civilization itself crawled back into the earth, deep down into the earth.

There are a few fragmentary documents left from that time, from the Mycenaean and the Hittite civilizations, that warn and worry about the destruction and mention The Sea Peoples. The Sea Peoples are coming, they say, The Sea Peoples bring death. The Sea Peoples are doing evil. The Egyptian civilization to the south noted The Sea Peoples as well. They heard rumors from their own envoys about what was happening. The Sea Peoples are on the loose, they heard. The Mycenaeans are no more. The Hittites are no more. The Sea Peoples ravage the lands. Get ready, the Egyptians were told, get ready for The Sea Peoples.

* * *

Did Rubens know about these things? He did not, is the answer. He didn't know about many of these things. How could he, even with all the volumes of classical literature falling off his tables? He didn't have the necessary archaeology. We have all the necessary archaeologies that Rubens was lacking. We can read the Hittite documents on their cuneiform tablets and the tablets with Linear B at Knossos as well.

Rubens couldn't rely on any of this archaeology, he didn't have the necessary material and so he didn't know. But then again, maybe he did know about these things. Maybe he had his own way of knowing. Something drew him to Silenus. Something made him think about Silenus and to paint him more than once. Something made him notice Silenus and portray Silenus with his knees and in his drunken and fat stumbling. Something made him see the message of futility in the person of Silenus. Some story of gloom going back all the way to The Sea Peoples was still alive enough that Rubens was able to see it and to portray it.

What does Silenus have to do with The Sea Peoples and the death and destruction of the old Mycenaeans and the ancient Hittites? Well, there is something. There is something that connects all this history, all these disparate thoughts. King Midas actually existed. That's the funny thing about the whole myth of Silenus and the friends of Dionysus. King Midas actually existed. It can make your mouth get a little bit dry when you think about the fact that King Midas actually existed, that he was an actual king. The stories are based on a real person, a real king. The myth of the capture of Silenus and the story about greedy King Midas and his lust for gold all go back to a real historical figure. He was a king before the days of Homer but after, long after the terrible events in which The Sea Peoples came from nowhere to fall upon a blighted land and make nothing out of something.

King Midas was a real man, I want you to understand that. We know nothing about him. But he was a real man. He built a real kingdom. He found gold in the rivers. The myths about King Midas and his magical powers of gold probably have to do with the fact that he really was a king and he really did have much gold. He filled his kingdom with gold. He was mad for gold just like the stories say. He found gold in the rivers and he draped it everywhere.

He was a Phrygian from the eighth century BCE, old King Midas. Who were the Phrygians? Well, they were the remnants of all the civilizations that got wiped away when the Hittites and Mycenaeans and the lesser empires collapsed. They were the people left over after The Sea Peoples came. They were a mixture of people who wandered into the blighted lands left over from The Sea Peoples and began to make a new civilization. The Phrygians were the next attempt, after the long dark period that comes after The Sea Peoples.

There is an ancient tablet written in the language of the Phrygians, in their own language, which is an Indo-European language just like ancient Greek and just like modern English. Anyone speaking modern English shares something, shares a direct linguistic line with the historical King Midas. On the tablet in the language of the Phrygians can be read the words, "Ates [?] dedicated and carved this stone for Midas, the protector of the people, the king."

He was the king and he was wrangling with the Assyrians to his east in Anatolia and they were all trying to rebuild the empires that had been lost when the Mycenaeans and the Hittites and everyone else went down hundreds of years before that. The Sea Peoples had wiped the slate of civilization clean, right down to the base again. There's barely anything to be found, civilization-wise, in the eastern Mediterranean, from around the twelfth century BCE until around the eighth century BCE when things get started up again. And the legend of King Midas is a memory from that period of the civilizational re-start. King Midas, with all his gold and his riches and his search for the secret of human happiness, is a man on the make for a civilizational rebuild. That's why he is so greedy. That is why he wants to know all the secrets. He's trying to rebuild something of glory after all the destruction and all the madness and all the tearing down of what had been built.

King Midas has heard all the stories of the Golden Age that came before him. Maybe he has seen some of the ruins from those old civilizations, the Mycenaean and Hittite remnants that still linger in the countryside and beneath the newer buildings tantalizing the new kings. King Midas is tantalized. That's why the stories of King Midas are the stories of a man possessed. He knows what is possible for humankind. He knows that something great used to be. He wants to know what it means to be great. And then Silenus tells him that the best thing for man is never to have been born at all and that the next best thing for man is, in the unfortunate situation that you have been born, to die as quickly as possible.

10. Nietzsche, the brilliant loner
    who would make a virtue
    and power and weapon of his
    loneliness, dreams of Silenus while
    masturbating.

NIETZSCHE, RUMINATING ON THESE matters beneath the walls of Metz as the guns of the Prussian army pounded the city, his mind in a kind of torment, realized that there was something profound going on with King Midas and Dionysus and with Silenus. He took it all so seriously that he stopped being a classicist. He quit the scholarly life. He walked away from the world, more or less. He took the horrible option. He took Silenus's option. He faced up to the hard thought and he decided that, indeed, it was true.

Did he think all of Germany was going to make the same decision, that everyone in the new nation of Germany was going to accept the truth of Silenus and embrace a new era of terrible youth? Probably he did for a short time, for the period of time in which he was enraptured by the music of Wagner as the new sound of the forest, the new goat music. In his enthusiasm,

Nietzsche accepted the idea that the best thing for man is exactly that, Nietzsche thought, to never have been born at all. Staying as close to that thought as you possibly can brings you close to the truth of everything. Nietzsche thought that, in a strange and seemingly paradoxical but not actually so paradoxical leap, staying close to that thought makes you powerful. No lies. That's the admirable side of Nietzsche. Not one fucking lie. Look at the terrible fact of life as squarely as you can, said Nietzsche. The best thing for man is never to have been born. Drink that thought in. Draw yourself up to the lip of the abyss. Know the full and complete and unavoidable desolation of that thought.

If you can do that, Nietzsche thought, if you can really do that, then a secret power comes to you. If you can stand at the center of utter desolation and say yes, then you have grasped an ancient virility. Nietzsche meant that very specifically. Virility. Power. He wasn't calling it power for nothing. To face up to what is best for man, that it is best for man never to have been born at all and, having been born, to die quickly, is to face up to the hardest thought and to have gained virility.

That's what Nietzsche tried to tell us, at least, and tried to believe in his own heart. But we can have our own doubts about this, as others have doubted what Nietzsche was trying to say, including Nietzsche's own friends and supporters and even including the one man to whom, for a time, Nietzsche gave his complete and utter admiration, that man being, of course, Richard Wagner.

The Drunken Silenus

If there is one man, Nietzsche thought, who is calling up in song the ancient powers of Dionysus then that man must be Richard Wagner. If there is one man whose music is, itself, a kind of thunderclap blasting through the bullshit then it is, Nietzsche cried out in worshipful fervor, it is and must be Richard Wagner. And then his great hero, the voice of Silenus in our time, as Nietzsche saw it, this man, this genius named Richard Wagner looked upon the figure of Nietzsche huddled up and spewing out mad and sometimes brilliant writings in one of his little hovels, his little hideaways tucked away in the Alps or wherever he was, and Wagner proclaimed that this writer, this prophet named Nietzsche was, in his deepest inner essence, a masturbator.

This upset Nietzsche. He wrote a whole book, Nietzsche did, a couple of years after Wagner called him a masturbator and he titled that book, basically, "I Hate Richard Wagner." But that's another story.

It is true, however, as Wagner seems to have noticed, that there is not a lot of human interaction in the writings of Nietzsche. There isn't much human-to-human physical contact. Sex, insofar as we mean the sexual act that requires at least two persons, that sort of activity is barely even hinted at in the writings of Friedrich Nietzsche except in a veiled and more or less disdainful sort of way. One wonders what Nietzsche thought that the satyrs and the nymphs and the other members of the Dionysian retinue were actually doing with one another out there in the forest. That part of it Nietzsche seems not to have wanted to think about.

For a man, in short, who wanted to take up the Dionysian thought that life is simply the expressing and expelling of a life force and nothing more, he doesn't leave much room in his analysis for the actual commingling of bodies. Aren't Dionysian bodies necessarily commingling bodies? Aren't they bodies compelled to penetrate one another in the brute physical sense of penetration? Isn't that part of the very drive, the desperate need to blast apart one's own individual being and to penetrate and be penetrated by another? Even the violence in Nietzsche is mostly of the implied sort. There is talk of power and the expressing and manifesting of power, but this power has an ethereal quality to it, like it is all happening inside of someone's head, which, of course, is exactly how the power of Nietzsche only ever existed, in his own head.

Noticing that Nietzsche seems unable to comprehend the penetrating and being penetrated part of the Dionysian madness, Wagner calls Nietzsche a dangerous and obsessive masturbator. This, you could say, puts masturbation in a rather bad light. But putting the relative merits of masturbation aside for a moment, Wagner's point seems to be that there are masturbators and there are masturbators and that Nietzsche was, shall we say, of the latter category, that's to say, a confirmed masturbator, a person who masturbates almost for the sake of masturbating. A person whose sole means of bodily sexual expression is of the masturbatory type.

The further implication, then, of Wagner's claim would be that when Nietzsche talks about the power that comes to those who accept the wisdom of Silenus and live without lies, that the power of those sorts of people comes in the desire, the fantasy of not ever, in no way ever in any situation needing anyone else. Never being tricked into needing another person. Being, in a full and complete sense, a masturbator in every single possible way.

The freedom of Nietzsche then consists, in a kind of onanism, which, it should be mentioned, Wagner discussed openly with Nietzsche's doctor and, probably, with a number of other people close to Nietzsche and, possibly, with Nietzsche himself. The point being that Wagner, in short, blabbed quite openly that he was worried that his little friend Nietzsche was an inveterate and dangerous masturbator and in these comments about Nietzsche's masturbation Wagner taps into what might be a rather deep point, a rather deep current in Nietzsche's understanding of the Dionysian truth, this being an understanding of life in which a person, perhaps an especially sensitive person who has been hurt many times by others, perhaps, a person, that is, just like Nietzsche himself, such a person is apt to fantasize that somehow, in some way or another, they will get revenge on all the people they ever needed or wanted by, finally, figuring out a way never to need or want anyone ever again. That, suggests Wagner, is the fantasy of the chronic masturbator, of which Nietzsche was one, and maybe not just one among many, but maybe one of the single greatest masturbators of all time.

Or, to put it another way, maybe what Wagner's comment shows us is that Nietzsche the Dionysian, Nietzsche the acolyte of Silenus, Nietzsche the Masturbator was really always just at war with love.

11. Jan Rubens experiences passion as love and love as death, which can make us wonder whether love is always in some core way connected to death. And beyond that, love and death are sometimes overseen by a strange power we might call historical grace.

JAN RUBENS WAS IN LOVE, AND THEN HE was on the run. Once the affair with Anna of Saxony was discovered and Jan was arrested, he ran back to his wife, Peter Paul's mother, begging her for forgiveness and for help. Who knows what was in the man's heart? Maybe the whole ordeal created deep within the soul of Jan Rubens a love of his wife that had never existed before. Maybe the fog of love was lifted from his eyes, the fog of lust cleared away and gone too was the clouding monomania that sets in when a married man runs into the arms of another woman. Maybe one passion had overtaken the mind of Jan Rubens as he fell into this desperate affair with Anna of Saxony, an otherwise difficult woman as the contemporary sources say, and it made him forget about the rest of the world. He started to see everything through the lens of this clawing need, the need to be with Anna of Saxony, the need to manufacture more and more reasons that he spend time with her, work on projects with her, center his life around her. This became a demanding and unforgiving logic. He stopped asking why, he stopped considering his life in any other light than the light of need. He needed to be with Anna of Saxony, dearest Anna, the only woman alive.

When the affair finally got busted up, Jan Rubens emerged from the experience as if waking up from a dream. Suddenly, that passion didn't seem real anymore. Suddenly, the insane drive to be with Anna of Saxony didn't even make sense. What had he been thinking? At that moment, the whole experience with Anna of Saxony might have seemed to Jan Rubens like an insane aberration. He might have found it extremely difficult to understand himself, although it had undeniably been his own self, that very same person, him, who had fallen down, down into the obsession with Anna of Saxony, a woman who now seemed to him so terribly flawed, who seemed to be a selfish and demanding woman, who seemed never to have been worthy of all that effort in the first place.

We can only imagine what it could have been like for Jan Rubens to go back to his own wife in shame and supplication. We can only imagine what may have happened in the interior of Jan Rubens, to his thoughts and feelings when he received from his wife,

Maria Rubens, a letter telling him that all was forgiven and that she would, in fact, stand by his side through all manner of worldly debacle. There is an astounding, you might even call it heroic, letter from Maria Rubens to Jan Rubens stating just such opinions. Or maybe it is a pathetic and weak letter, an embarrassing letter. It is hard to say. But the letter exists. It is part of the historical record. One part of me wants to call the letter heroic for the simple reason that it is so big of heart, so magnanimous, as they say. It is the kind of letter that only a person without the normal stores of anger and bitterness could write. That is what we can assume, at least.

In truth, it is impossible to know what motivated the letter. Maybe in some twisted and martyring way there is a form of revenge in the letter that Maria sent to Jan. Perhaps she gloried in her goodness. Maybe she lorded it over her husband, jabbing the fact of her own courage and fortitude into the soul of the man, a man who was deeply aware of his own cowardice, his own petty lusts. In fact, it is difficult to imagine that Maria Rubens was acting purely from the sense of a greater good, that her own capacity for big acts of spirit and generosity could have been of such astounding depth. So she will be a mystery to us, this Maria Rubens, as will so many women of that era, who have been erased except insofar as their lives touched upon the men in their lives, as will, in most ways, even Jan Rubens, and as will the specific thoughts of his son, Peter Paul Rubens, about his ruined father.

Jan Rubens. This is a man whose importance in history is as the father of a famous artist. We know the importance of this man. But it is an importance that isn't his. He is important as a bearer of someone else. Can a man ever fulfill himself simply by being the father of greatness? Is that enough? It is easy to feel an admiration for Jan Rubens simply for the fact that he did it, he produced a great son, a son about whom the world would marvel. He is to be admired for having done this, though it is not clear exactly what it is that he did. It is unclear whether there is any relationship at all between the specific attributes of a father and the accomplishments of the son. A terrible father can produce a great son or daughter. A great father will produce terrible offspring just as often as not. There is no clear relationship there. No one knows why.

Still, there is a real accomplishment simply in being the father of the man who would later paint the portrait of Silenus. Even if it isn't deserved. Even if the admiration cannot be linked to anything that Jan Rubens specifically did, the benefit comes anyway. In this, it has a similarity to the structure of grace. Grace doesn't come for a reason. If it did, it could be "earned." And earned grace wouldn't be grace. If you want grace, if you are trying to get it, then you see it as a reward and it is not a reward. The paradox of grace is that it has to come for no reason at all. Grace must come, sometimes, oft times, for the debased and unworthy. If it did not, it would have no meaning. And yet, the very fact that it comes to the debased and the unworthy threatens to make it meaningless, inscrutable to the point of being unreal. This is the hard thought.

Probably grace is something that resists too much thought. Do we see it, though? Do we see it in the world, the way that an impossible grace does seem to touch the people of the world in unpredictable ways? Do we? We see for a moment just what is happening and why, even though we lose the thought just as immediately, even though we can't bring it down enough to pick it apart and interrogate it. It escapes. Grace comes and then it escapes, before we were ever able to know it.

Maybe Jan Rubens is the recipient of a form of historical grace. Subsequent events in the life of his son give something backwards in history to Jan Rubens and transform him. He does nothing. He is dead when it all happens. Jan Rubens died in 1587. That is the end of the story for him. But it is not the end of the story. Peter Paul Rubens was born in 1577, so he was ten years old when his father died. Whatever the vague hopes in the mind of Jan Rubens, he died knowing nothing. He died a broken man, probably. He had denied his earlier Anabaptist leanings. He had fled Antwerp in the storms of the religious wars. He had struck up an insane affair with that woman, Anna of Saxony, all in the glow, we must imagine, of life and its possibilities. And then he was struck down. He was met with the ultimate test. Will you die for these things? Will you die for Anna of Saxony and the picture of life and its possibilities that you held in your heart? And he relented immediately. I recant, he said. I relent. I want to live. I want to be taken back into the life I had before. He broke. Jan Rubens broke and relinquished everything. He became then, we have to imagine, a thoroughly and completely broken man when he was released from prison and began to live with his family in Siegen where it was relatively safe, where he could hide from the ongoing storms of history that had been too much for him.

And then, flying in the face of everything he had actually done, anything he had actually deserved, Jan Rubens began to collect the un-hoped-for dispensations of grace. I suppose the first act of grace was a personal one. It was in the matter of personal relations, the way that individuals can suddenly rise up and become larger. Maria Rubens is just such a person, no matter how often we can suspect her, even doubt her. Did she have a devilish way of seeing ten moves ahead in the game of life and somehow calculating her way to an act of grace? Then it wouldn't be grace anymore, of course. Then we could take it away from her, we could snatch her grace back and call her the greatest devil of them all. She would be guilty of taking her husband's shame as a vehicle for her own greatness. She would be terrible, the most calculating woman imaginable.

Or maybe she was just weak. She wanted her man back and she was willing to grovel at the feet of princes and potentates and to forgive all the selfishness and pettiness of her own husband because she didn't have strength enough just to walk away. She was a woman, perhaps, trapped in her historical circumstances. She was a woman silenced and trapped and her only route forward was to try to rebuild, pitifully, the marital life that had existed for her before everything fell apart. What else could she do as a woman of the sixteenth century? And so her letter is just another sad document of what it means to be a woman in an era when being a woman was a kind of prison and cage.

But we cannot take it away from Maria Rubens, we can't take that letter away from her completely. The part that wants to distrust her in her moment of grace is overwhelmed by the fact of the thing. She did write that letter and, more importantly, she followed through on what it meant. That letter meant a life of pain and sacrifice for Maria Rubens. And that's the way it was. She wrote that letter and crawled back into the hole of suffering wifedom. In 1587 her husband Jan Rubens died, a forgotten man marked, at that point in time, by the disgrace of his entirely disastrous affair with Anna of Saxony, a disgrace (dis-grace) that led to his long imprisonment and to his renunciation of all the things he'd ever claimed to care about. So the letter is an act of supreme self-sacrifice.

But the letter is also an act of great defiance. She did it. She defied history. She defied the execution ordered by William the Silent. She defied the selfishness of her husband. There is a stubborn and immense power that can still touch one, through all the centuries, in that letter from Maria Rubens. She is still alive in that letter, while her husband, the cowardly Jan Rubens, is so very dead to us now. She, Maria Rubens, is the very vehicle

Jan Rubens experiences passion as love and love as death of grace, while he, Jan Rubens, is simply the undeserving recipient.

And then came the second act of grace, which was bestowed by the force of history in a backward-moving motion. Jan Rubens's son, Peter Paul Rubens, began to paint. And in painting Peter Paul found something. Peter Paul Rubens had a greatness in him. He painted, for instance, the Silenus painting. And from that painting it is almost as if the vapors from the oils and the chemicals themselves drift back into history and do the work of grace. Something goes back to the father and raises him up and redeems him. Suddenly, and in death, the father becomes a participant in that greatness although he has done nothing at all, although nothing has changed, although the facts of his life and his disgrace and his cowardly abandonment of everything he once stood for have not changed. Nothing has changed. But Jan Rubens has been changed. An act of historical grace has occurred.

12. All cities hide their horror.
Civilization itself can be seen as
the ongoing strenuous effort to
conceal shame.

THERE IS NO REASON TO KNOW
anything about Rubens or the friends of Rubens
or the age of Rubens when you walk around
the streets of modern-day Antwerp. The religious wars
are long gone. The occupation of the Spanish troops
is a memory that isn't there. The killings don't stain
the cobblestones anymore. Some of the old houses are
still there. But they recede. You have to go looking for
the memories and even when you go looking for them
they aren't always to be found. Even Ruben's house is
mostly a lie. The place had been completely forgotten
for a time. It had gone to rot. Parts of it were torn down.
No one remembers, anymore, exactly how it was all laid
out or what parts of it were meant to go where. Was the
kitchen right up in front like that? Probably not. Some
parts of the house were reconstructed from a half-assed
drawing made by someone who visited the house one
hundred years after Rubens was born. A person can
only wonder what might have passed through Rubens's

mind if you could show him what his house looks like now and how people walk through it in order to see how Rubens really lived.

The Plantin-Moretus house still stands. This house dominated Europe for a time in its way, dominated the written word. They were publishing books out of that house that defined what people knew. And now it sits there, telling its story just by sitting and passing time, waiting as the ages pass over it now with little effect.

All the old places of the world are repositories of the old stories and all the old stories are trauma. The entire history of the world is the history of an ongoing trauma and whenever you go to someplace new you can either decide to uncover parts of that trauma or to let it be. Most of the time we merely skate over the surface of a place, a city, a location in the world. We skate across the facades presented to us as the exterior. But with a little bit of digging the old stories start to come out.

The entire backdrop of the second half of the life of Peter Paul Rubens was, for instance, lived out during the time period of the Thirty Years' War. He painted the Silenus painting at around the beginning of what was to become the Thirty Years' War even though, at the time of course, no one could have known that the struggles between Hapsburgs and Bourbons and the continued fighting around issues of religion that had been unleashed by Luther's reformations were going to keep on going into a roughly thirty-year-long period of warring that would depopulate whole areas of what is now northern Germany. That war made a wasteland.

We can't see it now because it is very difficult to see a historical absence. It is very difficult to find and to see the places where history wore itself down to the bone. The Thirty Years' War was a work of destruction and of erasing. To look at it then was to look at ruins in the making.

There is no way to see the Thirty Years' War today. There is nothing that you can look at in modern-day Antwerp in order to get a look at the reality of the Thirty Years' War. The actual fighting of the Thirty Years' War never made its way to the city of Antwerp anyway. There is no specific destruction, therefore. And even destruction doesn't last as destruction. Destruction lasts as the thing that people do after the destruction in order to go on. You cannot preserve destruction. You cannot hold onto destruction. Destruction happens and then the people who are left after the destruction try to go on. There are layers of "going on" in a city like Antwerp that stretch over centuries and centuries. But they are masked, those layers, in the fact that when you are "going on" you want to do exactly that. You want to go on, so you obliterate the destruction. You destroy the destruction.

So, there is nothing especially to find in Antwerp when you walk around the corners and go into the little streets near the center of the town. These are the little streets of Europe that represent, as best as we can preserve it and fake it, the feel of these old cities as cities that do, in fact, tell a story going back into the period of time in which Rubens himself would have been walking around Antwerp during the time of the Thirty Years' War. Rubens walked these streets, indeed. And he did not. They are not his streets.

In fact, there aren't very many buildings that actually date from that era. Most things were destroyed. The buildings around the oldest squares of Antwerp are largely a pastiche of reconstructed facades that go back into the medieval days and into the renaissance days but most of them have been so changed and altered that you are seeing, mostly, the vision of what previous ages thought that the times before them would have looked like, or should have looked like. You are seeing the dream of the Middle Ages as it was dreamed by, say, the late eighteenth century, which, itself, is a period far enough away that we are able to dream about it. Dreams within dreams, and dreams upon that.

Walking around the streets of Antwerp is, then, a stroll through a complicated network of interlocking dreams. Every time the city has been blasted apart by war or upheaval or progress or natural catastrophe or anything else, the city has slowly attempted to put itself back together. It has tried to put the old parts of the city back together, either to improve them or to restore them back to what they were supposed to be, depending on the obsessions and fantasies of the period that is doing the putting-back-together. And so in making itself anew the city of Antwerp is constantly dreaming and re-dreaming dreams of what it had been.

In all the dreaming the traumas get suppressed, because these are waking dreams. In waking dreams you take present fantasies about olden times—fantasies that, no doubt, speak as much if not more about who you are than about what the olden days were actually like—and you start to fashion the actual look and feel of the city around you according to those waking dreams. The waking dreams of Antwerp are largely, it turns out, about peace and contentment. The imperial projects that were born within the confines of the city of Antwerp when it was the port that sent its ships out across all the seas of the world are no longer celebrated in the waking dreams of the dreamscape of the physical city of Antwerp. You hardly see reference to it at all. The religious wars that defined Antwerp and its place in the world for a century are nowhere to be found in any explicit manner on the streets or in the facades of the buildings in any obvious way in the older parts of town where the city of Antwerp dreams its dreams about itself. The pillage of distant lands is not part of that dream.

For hundreds of years vast mountains of goods came through the streets of Antwerp after being unloaded at the old docks and still today, even now, the goods come through, though quietly, in the port that has now been moved north of the city that has become a second city of shipping containers and the huge machines and shipping liners and trains and trucks that pick up these shipping containers and move the goods around the entirety of Europe. The story of goods and pillage is almost impossible to detect in the dreams of Antwerp that it tells itself in the squares and along the old streets that make up the oldest parts of this city of waking dreams that are being told and retold from age to age.

Antwerp is a peaceful city now, for now. It dreams about itself in the older parts of the city almost as if it really is asleep, as if it would in fact prefer to sleep, as if the gentleness that can be found on the daily walks you can take around the older parts of the city could be easily disturbed even if you spoke too loudly or jostled the blocks of the old buildings a little bit too hard.

Really it is war. Underneath the dreams there is unceasing war. The truth of Antwerp is war and murder. If the buildings of Antwerp were to portray themselves as they really are, it would be a story of war and murder written on their facades. Constant and ever-renewed war and murder. The streets of Antwerp are quiet and beautiful in the constant drizzle. But really they should be crying out about war and murder. They would cry out about the people running by, chased by an angry mob or by soldiers with leering, drunken faces pursuing human beings down the streets of Antwerp with the intent to kill. You can almost see the leering faces, the smile that comes welling up from deep inside a person when they have accepted the idea that they are going to rape and kill, hack and destroy and burn.

That is the story that Antwerp would tell of itself if not for the dreaming and the re-dreaming of the past that is always also a forgetting. The ships that came into the harbor and docked at the port of Antwerp were disgorging the booty of war and murder, directly or indirectly. The material testament to war and murder was streaming out from the docks and fattening the homes of the people of Antwerp for centuries. Even as the wars and the murdering of Europe, a continent of constant war and murder, were sweeping back and forth across the city of Antwerp for centuries the port was bringing back the loot from war and murder in places many of the people of Antwerp had never heard of and could never have imagined even in their wildest dreams. War and murder and nothing else.

13. In which the truth of strength is
found in weakness, the truth of
heroism in surrender.

I HAVE COME TO BELIEVE THAT RUBENS
loved Silenus. He loved the old man, the drunken
stumbler with his giant, though structurally
dubious knees. That is the secret. Rubens painted his
picture with sympathy, with understanding, and with
love. That is the primary difference between Nietzsche
and Rubens. Nietzsche saw the truth of Silenus but he
saw it as a hard truth, a truth that should make one hard.
Nietzsche saw Silenus in terms of his solitary and self-
enclosed hardness. Nietzsche saw Silenus as a fellow
masturbator. He saw Silenus as a heroic teller of truths,
the kind that demand heroic behavior. He admired the
Greeks for their ability, especially in the early days, to
look at the reality of life, look at the sheer discharge
of power that is the life force of creatures in their brief
existence and see that discharge as a truth beyond good
and evil.

Silenus, Nietzsche thought, shows us life as a sheer
expression of itself and nothing more, nothing less. Life
screams out, and then is extinguished. This screaming

out can be grand or pathetic, but to embrace it as such is to exist beyond good and evil. Beyond good and evil, thought Nietzsche, is beyond the categories we create for ourselves in our own fear. We fear the pure expression of life in its drive and in its pulsing need simply to be. We throw words over it, categories, judgments. We make up concepts like good and evil and then pretend that they mean something. All the while, life is seething up from its source and bursting forth and then dying away. A scream in the wilderness. A scream, a tussle, a death. Again and again. It is beyond good and evil, thought Nietzsche, beyond anything we can say about it. And Nietzsche looked to Silenus as the carrier of that truth, the truth of life beyond good and evil. The cry that goes up from the deepest glade in the forest, one beast falling upon another. The silence that echoes in the depths of the forest. Nothingness. And then strength out of that nothingness.

That's how Nietzsche saw it. But Rubens didn't see it that way. Rubens felt pity for Silenus and out of that pity came understanding. He felt pity and he felt it as a fellow sufferer. He saw a fellow sufferer and he began to love him. He began to love Silenus because there is nothing heroic in Silenus, actually. Rubens could not entertain Nietzsche's idea that Silenus makes us strong, that he was strong, that Silenus gives us access to the strength of Being in the acceptance of life as the discharge of power. Rubens never saw in Silenus a figure of strength in that way. Instead, he saw a figure that he could begin to love. Nietzsche was not capable of seeing Silenus that way because he was not capable of love.

Can we admit that, in reading Nietzsche, in spending a lifetime of reading Nietzsche, the thought suddenly springs to mind, "This man is incapable of love"? Or, at the very least, that he wanted to extinguish love, that he worked as hard as he possibly could to protect himself from the danger that is love. The idea that he could have uncovered the truth of Silenus and that this would have made him pity the figure of Silenus and then to love him would have seemed, to Nietzsche, the very antithesis of the truth the Greeks had discovered. Tragedy, Nietzsche would have objected, most assuredly has nothing to do with love.

Perhaps not. Perhaps Nietzsche was right about that, that there was no room for love in the initial impetus to tragedy.

The Greeks uncovered something vital, some vital force that connects us to real life and then we want to blunt that vital force with absurd discussions of love? Nietzsche, cock in hand, would not have been pleased. Silenus is a truth with which you can smash through the lies and return to something vital, he would have thought. You don't take a powerful force like Silenus and use him as a vehicle for pity. You most assuredly do not transform admiration for the great and harsh laughter of Silenus into a love of him. What right have you to love Silenus, Nietzsche might have asked us, fuming and incredulous. What right have you to dare to love Silenus? Silenus has revealed to you that the best thing for you, and for every human being is never to have been born, and having been born, to die as quickly as possible. That is the most honest answer to a question about life that has ever been given in the history of the world, Nietzsche would have said. And you respond with pity and then love? Nietzsche would not have been pleased by that idea. Nietzsche, terrified by love, would have been incredulous and quite possibly very angry. He was given to fits of anger.

Rubens, however, a man who came to the same truth of Silenus upon which Nietzsche later stumbled, did not hesitate in feeling pity for Silenus and then feeling love for Silenus. His painting of Silenus is neither in the heroic mode, as Nietzsche might have wanted, nor in the moralistic one, as the educators of the day might have preferred.

Silenus is not a symbol in Rubens's work. That ought to be said as well. The art historians are good at tracking down the symbols and reminding us about the associations of meaning that would have occurred in this or that time period and we are thankful to them for it. It helps to know these things. It helps to gain the context. You want to know what you are looking at and it is only possible to really know what you are looking at when you can read the signs.

Painters in Rubens's day filled their paintings with signs. That was something you did. It was expected. You can, if you would like, walk through the sixteenth-century section of any museum dealing with European art from that time and see yourself, in actuality, as stumbling through a vast and thorny forest of codes. Some of the code-work is obvious and some of the work is indecipherable, since the keys to the codes have been lost. If you walked through the museum thinking about all the codes you might suddenly come to the conclusion that while all the images around you seem to be of one thing, they are really about something else. The first layer is a feint, you might think. The first layer is a lie. What kind of world was this, you might wonder to yourself as you wander around this thicket of codes and double-speaking. Was everyone living behind masks? Was anything real? Is there anything true when the first layer of reality is a set of codes hiding another reality that lies beneath?

* * *

But Rubens was not interested in Silenus as a symbol, nor as a metaphor, nor an allegory. The way that Silenus stumbles out from the painting, seemingly heading off somewhere behind us, the viewer, somewhere off to our left, the impression that Silenus is quite possibly going to emerge from the painting and enter into the world of reality outside of the painting is something of a trick, of course. Rubens would have picked this technique out from any number of renaissance painters that came before him. The problems of perspective and distance had been worked on and a trained painter could, by the time of Rubens, engage in any number of painterly tricks in order to make a painted scene on a flat stretch of canvas take on all manner of three dimensionality and plenty of other things besides.

These were the tricks that the painters of Rubens's time had at their disposal. Rubens chose to use one of the tricks in his Silenus painting. He decided to use the trick where you erase, as much as possible, the impression of impermeability between the painterly scene and the actual reality inhabited by the viewer, wherever they may be. Sometimes you want to preserve that impermeability, enhance it even. Sometimes, as a painter, you want to make sure the viewer feels the distance, feels the way that the scene they are suddenly looking into is completely self-enclosed and completely removed in space and time and concept. The coherence of the painting might depend upon the fact that we see it in its unity, as something completely incapable of existing in the actual world that we inhabit as human beings viewing the painting from our reasonably concrete standpoint in the real world. The painting is one thing, one world, and we are another, and there is no possibility that those two distinct things could ever cross over into one another. The space doesn't connect. The worlds do not connect. The ideas do not connect.

But Rubens did not want to paint Silenus in that way. Rubens wanted to paint Silenus as if he could reach past that inviolable boundary that separates a painting from the real world. Rubens wanted the space to connect, the worlds to connect, the ideas to connect.

Rubens does one thing with that painting that always makes me feel vertigo when I think of it. He tilts the whole framing. It is dizzying, really, the effect. It makes you a little drunk and disoriented just to look at it. The whole painting is tilted on its axis and spilling down from the top of the canvas into the bottom. The entire scene, with Silenus and the satyrs and everyone else could come spilling out onto the floor at the foot of the viewer.

Silenus is not only stumbling around in the painting but stumbling around as if he will come careening out of the painting. He isn't stable inside the scene. He isn't even stable within the painting. He's coming out of there, maybe. In fact, the pinch Silenus is getting from the one black satyr may be a send-off. The satyr is holding Silenus by the upper bicep with one hand and pinching him with the other. Presumably, when the satyr lets go (is he going to let go right after the pinch?) that will be it for any semblance of stability, and Silenus will really tumble forward. Perhaps that will give him the extra momentum he needs to penetrate the boundary of the painting. The pinch gooses him up for one powerful final lurch, the downward slope of the painting spills everything to the bottom right corner. With the pinch and the release, the satyr is giving Silenus the final impetus that he needs to erase the impermeability of the line between the painting and the reality of the world in which the painting resides as a painting.

Silenus is coming. Silenus comes. There will be a great incarnation.

* * *

There's something else in the painting, something else that erases the boundary. It is a woman. She is standing behind Silenus next to the black satyr. She seems to be wearing a dark toga of some kind. Her skin is shiny and bright. Her hair is gathered and cinched up at the top of her head, revealing her entire face. She is looking right at us. She makes eye contact directly out of the painting.

What is the look on her face? How do you describe it? She is smiling, but it is a restrained smile. The cast of her face is conspiratorial. In that, she is like the satyr in the painting at the Mayer van den Bergh Museum. She isn't just looking at us; she is appealing to something in us. That is what she is doing. She knows us. She makes direct eye contact with us, looking from the painting and knowing that she will find us there. And she smiles, like the way that you smile at someone who is in on the joke, or to reassure them that they are in on the joke. She smiles at us, because she is with us and we are with her.

She must be a nymph. She is a nymph. A comely maiden in a scene like that can only be a nymph. She is a nymph staring at us from the painting, smiling knowingly and conspiratorially. Being a nymph, she might be of that specific class of nymphs associated with the trees, the dryads. She might even be one of the Hamadryades, the dryad nymphs specifically associated with oak and poplar trees and known to run with the Dionysian crowd, to be present in the circle of Silenus.

What does a Hamadryade know about us anyway? Why is she able to permeate the boundary of the painting and address us so easily? You are part of this story, she seems to be saying, yes you are. You are right here with us in the forest. You've known about the truth of Silenus all along. You don't need to be told about the condition of Silenus, she smiles at us with her head tilted to the side. Come over here, she smiles, or we will come over to you. It doesn't matter. She keeps her lips together when she smiles and she arches her eyebrows. She wants us to stop pretending. You know what is going on here. She knows that we know. She can hear the bleating of the goats and thinks that we can hear it too.

The nymphs are always associated with specific places, specific brooks, bubbling streams, groves of trees. The nymphs are found in the freshest places of nature gushing forth in new life, like a young girl just budding into womanhood. There is a nervous tension around a young girl like that. She is filled with that nervous tension and she projects it too. She makes everyone else nervous in being there at the cusp. When will she be fucked? Each moment that she is not fucked is like an eternity of nervousness. To associate nymphs with the idea of being oversexed is to miss the terrible urgency captured in the nymph, the just-about-to-be-fucked but the not-yet-fucked nature of the creature.

That is where a special kind of desire lurks, a desire that cannot be converted into specific thoughts. It has no language. Maybe at best it has a sound. Maybe you can hear some aspect of the desire of the nymph-about-to-be-fucked in the bleating of a goat. Maybe when Nietzsche asked what it means to think of God as a goat he was thinking of that, he was thinking of the bleat of a goat in the forest as a leering satyr pursues an about-to-be-fucked, orange-haired maiden nymph through a copse of trees in the darkest part of the wood. He may have been thinking of the look on the satyr's face and the look on the nymph's face and the sound of the bleating of a single goat, a goat who will, himself, soon be torn apart by the bare hands of the rest of the creatures and demi-humans in the party of Dionysus. There is a God in that, thought Nietzsche, the one true God.

Or maybe Nietzsche wanted to think that thought and it drove him crazy, drove him mad and made him feel that someone needs to be punished, that the world needs to be punished if for nothing else than that very need. Maybe he was driven crazy by the realization that we don't even know what we want from the orange-haired maiden, not really, and that she, equally, doesn't know, can't ever really know what she wants from us.

As Silenus stumbles and lurches forward, ready to spill down into the bottom-left-hand side of the canvas, as he is revved up by the pinching and goosing of the satyr who sends Silenus forth to penetrate the boundary of the painting, we are invited in by this nymph, who erases all distance we might have kept from the scene. She implicates us in the scene, you might say. She assumes things about us as she beckons us into the scene. She smiles at us conspiratorially, knowing that we are already there, that we understand something about goat noises. She isn't afraid of us, though we are a little bit afraid of her.

14. The conundrum and unsolvable mystery of Maria Rubens and her pen. The desire that hides behind desire.

IWOULD NOT BE SURPRISED IF IT WAS that letter from Maria Rubens to Jan Rubens that finally broke him completely. She accepts his apology, first of all, and then she goes on to mildly rebuke Jan for considering that she might have done anything else. What power there is in that statement from Maria. She is telling Jan something about solidity. She has solidity and he does not have solidity. It isn't even hard for her, she seems to be saying. And now, through the sole cause of her husband's immense folly and the single-minded passions through which he pursued an insane dalliance with Anna of Saxony, through that cause alone, Maria will now suffer and she will do so willingly. Jan Rubens tried to take her power away and now she is going to take it back again. She is going to take it back by willing the thing that was, initially, beyond her control. She has control of it now.

They go back to being Catholics at that point. The Anabaptist impulses fade away. Jan surrenders back into Catholicism. They know that Jan can never again be a person of any substance or solidity in the world. He gave up the possibility of substance when he decided to pursue Anna of Saxony to whatever end. He wasn't calculating about ends, then. He was simply pursuing. Perhaps he told himself strange and outlandish stories about how it would turn out for the best somehow, that he would be taken up by the power and influence of the lady of Saxony.

But she was married to William of Orange, William the Silent. They called him William the Silent because he kept his silence for a long time. The silence was not about his wife's affair with a Flemish lawyer. William kept silent about plans for wholesale murder, for the slaughter of tens of thousands, hundreds of thousands. (Is there a history to be written of all the mass murders that almost occurred, all the horrors over and above the actual horrors, all the horrors that were just barely averted?) William the Silent had heard talk. William the Silent was privy to discussions between the Duke of Alva and King Henry II of France. The Bourbon power and the Holy Roman Hapsburg power, the two old rivals were going to get together in order to take care of a mutual problem. This is true. Don't take this as a story. It is important that it is true. Henry and the King of Spain, Philip II, were planning to murder all the Protestants. They were going to wipe France and the Netherlands clean of all the Protestants. They were going to end the religious and political strife through a sustained campaign of killing, utter extermination. That was the plan, anyway.

William heard all of this talk, but he kept his silence. So, once the story of William of Orange's silence made the rounds, people started calling him William the Silent, in recognition of that remarkable act of keeping silent.

Why did he keep silent for so long? No one knows for sure. Probably he was scared and overwhelmed. Probably, too, he was always a silent one, always the type to bide his time until the way forward became clear. The fact that he did eventually take action makes the title "William the Silent" dignified in the end, admirable, if in incomprehensible ways.

Slowly and quietly, William mounted a campaign of political and then military resistance to the forces of the Hapsburg Empire and to the Catholics and to the Spanish troops that were the armed wing of the Hapsburg Empire in the Low Countries. These are all matters of history, the complicated intrigues of the day. These were the forces of history into which Jan Rubens inserted himself when he decided to pursue Anna of Saxony, wife of William the Silent during the time of the great religious wars.

We don't know anything specific about what went on between Jan and Anna, about the plans that they hatched together late at night when they were, supposedly, going over the legal matters of her estate. We don't know the dreams and plans they may have cooked up together. Somewhere, though, in the back of

Jan's brain must have lurked the realization that these plans with Anna of Saxony were nothing, fantasies. There must have jumped into his brain sometimes late at night a feeling of panic, a feeling that he was spiraling into the abyss, into nothing. There was no endgame, no realistic endgame for Jan and Anna. It is hard to imagine a scenario where they were not aware of this fact in some form, where this awareness did not, on occasion, burst through the madness of their pursuit of one another. Perhaps it was the case that day in and day out they told themselves and one another that this was the last day, that the thing would have to an end on that very day. We don't know. We don't know the details of the pursuit.

We have information that Anna of Saxony was, previous to her affair with Jan Rubens, angered by her knowledge of the indiscretions of her own husband, William the Silent. This knowledge, this anger, may have given her a sense of license. She may have felt that she had earned her own right to violate the bonds of matrimony. She may have seen something in the eyes of her lawyer, Jan Rubens, that struck her as an opportunity for a kind of revenge. Or, stories of her husband's amorous adventures may have given her a feeling of righteousness that was a necessary element in her motivations to go through with something she wanted to do anyway. The entire affair might have been temporary. Jan and Anna might have thought of it as a temporary dalliance that would not, that could not last. They simply got carried away. They took it too far and it went on for too long. Suspicions were aroused and Jan and Anna fooled themselves into thinking that suspicions were not aroused.

In the crazy logic of the pursuit, they became blind to the fact that everyone around them was aware of what was going on. They lied to one another. They kept a fantasy alive for the simple reason that they could not stop. Something else, some other force had hold of them and was driving the thing forward. It wasn't possible to stop anymore. They kept giving one another reasons why it could continue for another day, always another day. They would have looked out of the window in Anna of Saxony's study at a tree in the courtyard and it would have seemed so alive, that tree. The greenness of it would have been overwhelming, the way that a breeze was caught up in the leaves as if something were animating the branches.

Eventually there was one day too many. A disgruntled servant, a member of the household looking for privilege through the divulging of information, a loyal confidante to William, someone, we don't know who it was, but someone finally decided to take action. Somehow, news reached the ears of William of Silent that could not be ignored. Anna and Jan denied the affair for some time. Anna claimed that there was no proof and she wanted the accusations taken to a court of law. Then it became clear that she was pregnant. Since her husband, William of Orange, had not been physically present at the house where Anna stayed that year, there was no debating. A girl child was born in

August of the year 1571. She was named Christina. She was, in fact, the half-sister of Peter Paul Rubens, who would be born six years later, after the imprisonment of Jan Rubens, after his near execution, after his return to Maria and his acceptance that his life as a man of the world, a man of any consequence at all, was over.

Anna and her daughter Christina were effectively banished. They were sent to a castle where they were kept in isolation. Anna began to suffer mental and physical breakdowns. Her marriage to William the Silent was annulled. Finally, Anna was moved to Dresden and put into a room with no windows and a slot through which she received her daily allotment of food. By most accounts she became completely insane. Taken from the world, she lost contact with it. She lost contact with herself and everything else besides. In the year 1577, the very year that Peter Paul Rubens was born to Jan and Maria, Anna of Saxony died in her one-room cell in Dresden. She was thirty-two years old.

So, those were the stakes. Jan and Anna could not have known, of course, that those would be the exact stakes. But they must have known that those were, roughly, the stakes. They must have known that their situation was roughly that dangerous. Jan spent several years in prison and during a part of that time it seemed that he would soon be put to death. It was only after the constant and repeated lobbying from Jan's wife Maria that William the Silent decided to let Jan live and then later to release him from prison. But Jan had to pay various fines and was prevented from re-entering anything like the normal life he had enjoyed before the affair with Anna.

The potential outcome of the affair between Anna and Jan was going to be, they must have known, death. Death was a potential outcome. And if not death, then another potential outcome was the complete destruction of life as both of them had known it. For Anna, it would be the ending of her marriage to an extremely powerful and prominent person. The ending of a marriage like that comes with consequences. She would have realized that.

For Jan, a potential outcome of the affair with Anna would be the end of his marriage and the end of his career, a career in which he had carefully built up a network of alliances and associations with powerful people, a career in which he had tried to navigate between the various and complicated forces of his time in Flanders. The tensions of all of Europe were tearing Flanders apart during the time when Jan Rubens was trying to make a public life. The tensions of a Hapsburg Empire trying to hold onto the regions of Northern Europe going up into the Low Countries. The tensions of the Protestant Reformation and the Counter-Reformation. The normal tensions of business and diplomacy. All these tensions. And Jan Rubens had been very careful and principled in his attempts to navigate these tensions and to make a public life for himself. But his affair with Anna of Saxony was not at all like that. It was not careful, nor was it principled. It simply took its course. It simply took its course and the course went careening toward death.

The outcome might very well have been death right then and there, very quickly after the affair was discovered and confirmed by William of Orange. But William of Orange was a careful and calculating man himself, as we know from the fact that he came to be called William the Silent. He was accustomed to hearing terrible and disturbing things and then taking his good council on these matters. William the Silent was a listener and a thinker, that is what he was doing in his silence. He was figuring out ways. He had his own diplomatic reasons for marrying Anna of Saxony in the first place. He wanted alliances with the powers of Germany during the times of the religious wars and the troubles with the Hapsburg Empire. He saw the angles. He had been silent, but he had plotted and strategized all along. His wife's execution and the execution of her lover would be a traumatic and controversial matter during delicate times. So, Anna and Jan did not meet their deaths right then and there. Anna would meet her death slowly, in stages of isolation that were to take the world away from her until she had nothing left. With nothing at all, she went mad. The nothingness was a madness to her. The madness was a sickness that carried her away. Within six years of her affair with Jan Rubens, she was dead.

For Jan, the world was taken away simply by placing him back within it with no prospects, no hopes, no opportunity to rebuild the life that he had led up until the point when he met Anna of Saxony.

That was what Maria Rubens, Jan's wife, heard and understood. When Maria wrote to Jan in prison in order to forgive him she was fully aware of the situation. Her response was to accept those conditions absolutely, to will them to be her own conditions, to take upon herself the devastation of life that Jan had taken upon himself in his madness, in his pursuit of Anna of Saxony into the face of death. Jan pursued Anna of Saxony into the very maw of death and then did not enter. Death was not given to him.

In a sense, he received something worse than death. He came to know that he had taken up a pursuit into the face of death for no reason at all, to no purpose that he could now divine, sitting in his jail cell and writing letters to the wife who now represented his single and only connection to life and the world. Having run up into the jaws of death and then been spit back again into the world, his only connection to that world was in the person who represented his shame. Jan was reduced to having one thing, his wife Maria. She was also the thing he had thrown away in his mad dash toward Anna of Saxony and toward death. He had fallen in love with Anna of Saxony in a sort of burning way, a way that would destroy the entire world if that were the cost, probably. Probably Jan Rubens and Anna of Saxony would have set whole cities aflame were it to their benefit.

We don't know the ends to which they would have gone. We do know the stakes though. And we have the reasonable assumption that they would have been aware of the stakes. And that the stakes were death was of no matter to them. It could not affect their pursuit. It could not deter. It meant nothing that they were running into the very abyss of death. That fact made Jan and Anna of Saxony run faster. They galloped toward death and then were stopped at its threshold and thrown aside. When Anna of Saxony finally got her death, the death no longer held any meaning. She couldn't understand it anymore. It was no longer the thing toward which she had been running.

When Jan Rubens finally got his death it was after many years of life as a broken man. He would have been a man broken down and given to a life's project of forgetting and to the small, daily pleasures that are left to someone who has thrown away his dignity and his honor for something he can no longer understand. Sitting in prison and writing to his wife, Jan Rubens would have lost touch with any understanding of his run to death with Anna of Saxony. The understanding comes in the running. The running toward death is itself an act of meaning, it creates the understanding through which the running is possible. When the running stops, everything evaporates. The understanding melts into the ether. The mind has nothing to hold onto. Suddenly the burning path toward death is transformed into a desolation. When the running into death was over, everything was over. Fear entered back into his heart, fear and a desire to live.

In the name of fear and a desire to live, Jan Rubens sat down at his desk in his prison cell and began to compose a letter to the wife he had left behind. He wrote to her a plea for life in his desolation, the gates of death having been closed to him. Did he hope for anger from Maria, for renunciation? We don't know. Did some part of Jan Rubens hope that he would be punished by Maria to the exact degree of intensity with which he had been driven mad by Anna of Saxony? Anyway, he wrote to his wife.

She responded with a terrifying letter of acceptance and self-renunciation. She would take him back without conditions, without regrets, and without resentment. It is impossible to know what conversations were had between Jan and Maria in the privacy of their own home after the letters had been sent and read and new letters sent and new letters read, after Jan was finally released from prison and the dangers of the moment had passed. It is impossible to know how Maria really felt about her decision after the fact. We know that Jan did, actually, remove himself from any active participation in the world upon his release from prison. He resigned himself to a life of basic and nameless toil. He raised a family. He became a father to Peter Paul Rubens and to Peter's other siblings. He died to the world.

But maybe he was reborn too. Maybe he saw something after all, after the running to death and then the fear and then the humiliation and the pathetic return to Maria in the face of nothingness. Maybe something was given to Jan Rubens in the renunciation and the surrender that defined his life after he was thrown into prison by William the Silent. He was forced to beg for his life. More than that, he was forced to allow his wife to beg for his life. His life was in danger because he had betrayed his wife in a mad dash for death with Anna of Saxony. He had grabbed the hands of Anna of Saxony and the world had opened up for him in shining ways that had made everything else seem pale and lifeless in comparison. Jan Rubens and Anna of Saxony had taken leave of all the normal rules at that point. They were not obeying the normal rules anymore. They would follow their own set of rules, the only thing that seemed real. And they would run forward in a mad dash for death, if that be the end result. So be it. Death, death and reality, death and truth, death and love. And then it was taken from them. And the world turned again. The reality of death and truth and death and love began to seem like a dream. And then they became fearful. They were filled with shame and regret.

Jan Rubens returned to his wife in shame and regret and the desire to live. He begged for her forgiveness and then he consented to the idea that she would, in turn, become a supplicant in his name. She, Maria, the one who had been betrayed by the mad dash for love and truth, would now, in turn, beg forgiveness in the name of the one who had betrayed her. Jan allowed all this to happen. He willed it in his fear and in his shame. He allowed the wife he had betrayed to beg William the

Silent for his life. He must have obliterated himself in that moment of consent. He reduced the entirety of his hopes and dreams and ambitions to a cinder and then he burned that cinder into a vapor and the vapor was gone. There can have been very little left of Jan Rubens, a hunk of flesh rotting away in a prison cell. A man, sure, but not really. From where could he have drawn any substance? Nowhere. He had reduced himself to a vapor and that vapor had blown out of the window on a cold morning in what was later to become Germany, from the window of a prison cell, blown away.

Did Jan Rubens learn something vital at that moment of absolute reduction? Did he gain something in giving everything away? Maybe a hugeness entered into the soul of Jan Rubens at the moment that he gave everything away, gave himself away, surrendered to the idea that he was nothing at all, a vapor. Maybe that was something Maria saw, too. Maybe she understood something about it, something impossible to express. Maybe she offered her husband the opportunity to be erased and then to find something in the void.

If Jan Rubens saw something, if he found something in the void of himself then he would have kept that quiet. It would have been something that you don't need to tell. It would have been something that he shared with Maria as their own secret, a small secret about life that only exists because you do not tell it to the world, you cannot tell it to the world. You have found something real in the abyss, when you transformed what you thought was your most important self into a vapor and then released the vapor into the void. And when the vapor drifts away you are reborn. You keep this rebirth as a secret. Maybe that was a secret that Jan and Maria shared after the collapse. Maybe it was something, a gift that came to them because of the collapse, that could have only been given to them because of the collapse. Maybe Maria understood that fact after all. She knew that something huge, a huge and incommunicable secret had presented itself as a possibility for herself and her husband Jan.

How many people get the opportunity to collapse completely? How many people get the opportunity to test themselves in a run toward death and a brief glimpse of the abyss? How many people get the opportunity to erase themselves into a vapor and then find out what happens next? Maybe Maria understood this and guided Jan along and then he was able to understand it too, to understand the opportunity hidden in the terror.

15. The hardness of Silenus transforms into pity, the pity of Silenus and the pity for Silenus. Nietzsche is not amused.

NIETZSCHE DOES NOT SPEND MUCH time, in *The Birth of Tragedy* or anywhere else, fleshing out the character of Silenus. Silenus represents, for him, the capacity for the ancient Greeks to realize the sheer horror of existence. The Greeks, Nietzsche thought, spent some time facing up to that horror. The way Nietzsche tells the story, when Silenus is first captured by King Midas, Silenus presents himself as stern and immovable. He isn't interested in telling King Midas anything. He stonewalls the king. He has a strength, a dignity. Finally, after repeated urgings from King Midas, Silenus gives in. The way Nietzsche explains it, Silenus finally decides to tell King Midas what is best for man with crazed glee. Silenus bursts out with a shrill laugh. He laughs at the king and then reveals to him that the best thing for man is never to have been born at all and that the second best thing for man is to die as quickly as possible.

The Drunken Silenus

Silenus represents two things for Nietzsche: He is the hard truth of the horror of existence, and he is the mad and gleeful acceptance of that horror in the sheer discharge of life. Nietzsche imagines that Silenus would respond to King Midas first with the silence of contempt and then with the laughter of contempt. The old king, Silenus thinks in Nietzsche's version, is able neither to grasp the fact that existence is horror, nor that there is a possible celebration of life in its sheer discharge that is to be experienced on the other side of that horror.

It is hard, though, to imagine Rubens's Silenus laughing in that way. It is hard to imagine the hardness. Rubens's Silenus is soft and flabby. He is broken down. He wouldn't stonewall King Midas in that way. He would remain silent for some time, sure. He wouldn't know whether it makes any sense to speak or not. He would be wary. He would be unsure of himself in the face of this insistent king. Maybe, even, he would feel sorry for King Midas. He would understand that the king is desperate for knowledge. He would understand that King Midas, the great King Midas, has scratched and clawed his way into worldly greatness over an entire lifetime of noble, and also of ignominious and hateful, deeds. King Midas has done it all. He has killed and loved and plotted and risked. He has lived in the world. He has dared to put his own existence on the line again and again for glory. He threw calm and ease away. He renounced calm and ease in order to be the greatest of men among men.

The Silenus that Rubens portrayed in his painting would have been aware of the aching desire in the king. King Midas was still searching, still looking for secrets. Just look at the way that King Midas phrases his question. The question is posed perfectly there on the cutting edge between selfishness and altruism, between desire and ethics. He doesn't ask, "How can I be the most powerful king ever?" He doesn't ask, either, "How can I be a good man?" He threads a needle between the two ideas, he outflanks both questions with a clever and ambiguous phrasing that can mean both and neither at the same time. What is the best thing for man? What is the best and most desirable thing for man?

It is almost as if Old King Midas fully suspects that the answer will be a mockery of the very question. In threading the needle, in asking such a carefully phrased question, King Midas shows that he is aware that there is a problem in asking the question at all. He wants to be very careful, even though he is the great and powerful king. He wants to be careful to ask the question in a way that does not reflect badly on him. But he also wants something he can use. He wants knowledge that will give him more power. And yet, the fact that he wants to know what is best for man shows a hesitation in the face of worldly goods. He has tasted so many worldly goods. He has known many of the things that are supposed to make a man happy. He has fucked and killed and intrigued and planned and warred and plotted. He has acquired great riches. But it is not enough. The fact of it drives him further and further. Nothing is enough. He wants to know why. He is searching for Silenus because he wants something more. But what? He is cautious even in his wanting.

He realizes, despite himself, that he may be asking the wrong question. He has come to the end of a line, the end point of his way of living. He wants to go somewhere else but he is scared to go somewhere else. All these doubts and worries, they are there in his question, written all over him. He isn't sure, anymore, how to get what he wants because he isn't sure what to want. It is almost as if he has long come to suspect that there is no such thing, no thing that is best and most desirable for man, that the very situation of having no possible answer to that question is the situation in which men live and die and ever will.

When Silenus tells the king his truth, it must come as a confirmation of fears and suspicions long held. Because the answer is that there is nothing you can desire that will make it all okay. There is nothing to be desired, no good that can come of your existence that will have made all the suffering understandable. There is nothing like that to be found. The bearer of this message, as Rubens understands it, would have much to carry. We can imagine Silenus, through Rubens's eyes, relating the fact of the best thing for man in a soft voice. There might be a hint of malice in Silenus's eyes while he talks. There may be a glimmer of drunken anger. King Midas has forced him to speak, after all. King Midas, for all his searching, is willing to hurt and deceive in order to get what he wants. King Midas has tricked Silenus and captured Silenus and now, finally, is about to get some information that will, purportedly, be of direct benefit to him even if, in his heart of hearts, the king suspects that his question is going to result in profound disappointment.

Silenus has understanding and compassion for King Midas, along with a certain amount of contempt. He speaks his truth softly, but with a smoldering anger, a smoldering contempt for anyone unable to come to this truth on his or her own, unable to see the truth screaming out in the reality that they confront. But when he is finished speaking, Silenus feels only sadness. The end result can only be a certain amount of sadness. The deed is done. The truth has been spoken. The demigod can go back to the Dionysian milieu, back to where the cycle of frenzy and collapse repeats itself again and again and again.

Is the Silenus that Rubens paints in his painting that very Silenus, the Silenus trudging back into the Dionysian milieu after having spent his time with King Midas? Maybe that is why the satyrs are giving him the extra cajoling. They are pinching him and heckling him because he has just been captured by a king and returned by a king. They are happy to have him back but they are happy to tease him as well.

"Ah Silenus," they are saying, "how did you let the old king get hold of you?"

They know the answer of course. The king trapped Silenus by turning a stream into wine. King Midas trapped Silenus in the same way that Dionysus keeps Silenus. The haze of drunkenness is the thing that imprisons Silenus, that captures him. Silenus is powerless before it. That is to say, he is powerless before the truth that it is his burden to keep. The truth of Silenus—that the best thing for man is never to have been born and the second best thing for man is to die as quickly as possible—that truth is kept in a safe place within Silenus's everyday mind by the careful and assiduous application of alcohol. It is a thought, Silenus's truth, that must be kept floating in a vat of alcohol at all times, only to be brought out in times of crisis, in times when it actually must be confronted as a reality. Silenus, after all, is immortal. He is one of the deathless ones. And yet he lives a worldly life, an otherwise mortal life that simply goes on forever. Sometimes Silenus would prefer to die. He grabs for his cups. He pushes the thought away.

One implication of the terrible wisdom of Silenus, after all, is that it is, in fact, a blessing for humankind to have been given the gift of death. There is an end to the worldly sojourn for man. There is an end to the endless cycle of life in nature for man, and that end is found in death. The fact that life is meaningless is, for Silenus, a fact that must be encountered on a daily basis forever. Silenus is doomed to witness the repetition ad infinitum. His revelation of the truth to King Midas must, then, come with a certain amount of bitter reflection. Human beings may not realize that the best thing for them is to die, they may be overwhelmed by the truth of this thought, but they are going to get it anyway. They are going to get their death, every one. The death is coming. That it is good, that it is to be wished for, may be the hardest thought of all, may be the thought that is left unthought by the vast majority of human beings as they pass through life into the death that waits. But it awaits nonetheless.

The secret message hidden in Silenus's otherwise shocking and destabilizing truth is that the thing that awaits, the death, the annihilation that awaits is, in fact, the answer. The good lies within that fact somehow, lies within the fact of the absolute certainty of death. The only possible goodness that can be said to exist in the endless cycle of life is, then, seemingly paradoxically, the fact of death. The very best thing, Silenus says, is never to have had to endure it in the first place, to have been thrown into the separation from death that is coming to life. But once a person has been separated from death in being born, in coming to life, the very best thing after that is to know death after having lived a life.

Silenus knows this better than anyone. He knows it because he bears witness day after day. He bears witness to the endless cycle of life and knows very well that there are no answers to be found within the relative length or brevity of that cycle for any one individual. Living a little bit longer or a little bit shorter doesn't change anything. When it comes to the question of death, the simple fact of being born throws a person into the dilemma. It is being born that initiates the problem of death. So, in a sense, the best thing for man is not to be born at all. That's to avoid the problem altogether. But once you have been born, you enter into the pain of life, a pain that is made acute because it is structured to end in an incomprehensible death. The great cycle of life and death, which in its very continuance has a kind of logic and purpose, is not experienced as logical and purposeful by the individual beings who do the actual work of living and dying. But the cycle of life demands that there be this work of living and dying. The cycle of life preserves the meaning of the whole. But it does so through the individual deaths of the members who constitute the cycle of life. Dying is a wretched and empty thing in itself. Having been born, Silenus suggests, the best thing would probably be simply to complete the circle, to play your part in the infinite and incomprehensible cycle of life. To die.

If you want to find some meaning, Silenus suggests, then you will find it in the fact that life is for the purpose of death and death is for the purpose of life. If you are troubled, Silenus tells King Midas, by the condition in which you find yourself, a mortal facing your own mortality, then you ought to look to the greater cycle. That is what you serve. You serve the cycle. In serving the cycle, you will die. Living thing, you are for death. Death is the thing that you move inexorably toward. Run to it, Silenus suggests. You might as well run to it. It calls you there. It calls you toward it. You want to know what the best thing is for you, living man. Serve the cycle. There it is for you. Your own death, waiting. Run to it quickly. And die.

* * *

The hardness of Silenus transforms into pity

Silenus cannot die. He walks heavy on his massive haunches, unable to die. Does he feel envy for King Midas? At least King Midas is able to die, at least he is able to fill out the cycle and run toward death.

Maybe that is why Rubens has such compassion for Silenus. He sees Silenus as man-like. He sees Silenus as one of us. Silenus is close to the mortals. He doesn't have the strange indifference to mortality that you see in the other gods. Look at Dionysus, even, the way Titian painted him leaping from his chariot toward Ariadne. This thing, this deity, is not concerned with mortal things. He has another structure for his experience. He cannot be understood, cannot be approached. His way of being is completely other. He has no understanding of death. And death is the thing that, at its core, structures human experience. It is the mechanism at the heart of what it means to be human.

What is being human without being finite, without losing time, without the memory of past experience and the movement toward the cessation of all experience? It is nothing. We can't understand it. The idea of an infinite being is the idea of a being that cannot ever be understood. The experience is too far away. It can't even be called experience.

But Rubens understands Silenus. To understand him, he makes a mortal of him. In the painting, Silenus stumbles forward like a man, awash in the troubles of finitude. In fact, Silenus has no finitude. He participates in time in a different way. He is of the deathless ones. But his wisdom is of finitude. He is obsessed with finitude.

You could say, almost, that he is the god of finitude. That is how Rubens paints him. Silenus stumbles in a drunken lurch, lurching out of the painting that cannot hold him because he is thick with our greatest problem. He took it up. He took up the human problem. For whatever reason, Silenus decided that the human problem was his own problem even though he doesn't experience the human problem as such. He made it his problem.

That, I suppose, is where Silenus becomes Christ-like for Rubens. There is a glimmer of the Christ in Silenus because Silenus is the divinity who would become flesh, who would take on the burden of mortality, of living and dying as a common man. He stumbles out of the painting because he wants to be born into our world in order truly to experience the problem of finitude. He wants to know and to experience the reality of living and dying. He seeks an incarnation. Silenus's immense sympathy for King Midas is evident even in his anger and sarcasm. Even in his disgust with the willful ignorance and stupidity of King Midas, Silenus loves him enough to tell him the most profound truth he knows, one of the most profound truths that has even been spoken to man. Rubens understood that sympathy. Rubens understood that Silenus wanted to become man in order to feel the problem of living and dying. So Rubens painted a picture that is a return of that sympathy. Rubens decided that he would love Silenus in return for the love that Silenus felt for the condition in which he found all creatures.

16. There is something special and different about the gods who die. Or, to put it another way, a true god must die.

WHY DOES SILENUS STAY WITH Dionysus anyway? What does it mean for a god to have a tutor, to have a caretaker? It is as if Silenus sees Dionysus as a child. It is as if Dionysus wants to be seen as a child. Actually, that is the truth of it. Dionysus is the child god. He is the baby god, the god that grows and dies and is reborn and then goes through the whole process again and again. He doesn't just die, he is pulled apart, hacked apart limb from limb in some of the stories. He is the god who is murdered and then put back together and reborn. That does not happen to the other gods. The other gods come to be all of a sudden and then simply are. Or they have always been and always will be. The other Olympians are more permanent, more static.

In the mystery rites that the Greeks used to celebrate, the birth and death, the murder and rebirth, the killing and resurrecting of Dionysus, was enacted. It was played out in ritual form. Goats were put to the sword after having been coerced to give their own tacit consent to the murder about to happen. They were made to shudder or to cry out. A priest of the rites would splash the goats with cold water. And the goat would shudder and bleat. The ancient Greeks heard this as the cry of Dionysus.

"We goats are ready to die. Kill us now."

A lingering whiff of human sacrifice can be smelt in the ancient rites of the Greek mystery cults. Before the goats, these people killed men, it seems. What were they doing in those caves and grottoes? What was this about the child that had to be torn apart so that he could be remade again? What is it about the giant cauldron, the three-legged cauldron stewing away in the dark and sacred places? The smell of flesh is bubbling up from the three-legged cauldron. There is goat in the cauldron; there is lamb in the cauldron. Is there something more in the cauldron? No one wants to talk about what might be floating around in the cauldron. It is not to be spoken of.

Dionysus must die and Dionysus must be reborn. Thus is he the god of the cycle. Life is death and death is life and all of that and so forth. The murder of Dionysus is the eventual rebirth of Dionysus. Somewhere in a cave above the plains in Greece during the ancient times, a group of people circle around a trembling goat and chant the rites of Dionysus. They are drinking wine from ritual cups and driving themselves into a frenzy that will end in death. The beast will be split open and the hot blood will be spilt upon an altar. More incantations will issue forth from human mouths, the sound mingling with the death cries of the goat. The smell must be incredible. The smell of hot blood and human bodies worked up in terror and exhilaration. The meat of the goat goes into the cauldron. Soon, a communal meal will be had, a sharing of the feast coming directly after the shared act of killing. Some of the pieces of flesh from the dead animal will be wrapped up in another goatskin. The god is being put back together again. The dead flesh is to be made into the flesh of life eternal. Dionysus, the god who was sewn into the thigh of Zeus after his mortal birth. He must be born mortal and again born immortal. He must live and die and live again.

* * *

Dionysus needs a tutor because Dionysus is the god who dies. He experiences childhood. Dionysus must go through the cycle of life and death forever. He must grow and die and be killed and be reborn and grow and die and be killed again. And so Dionysus, the child god, needs a caretaker. He of perpetual life and death needs a tutor of perpetual life and death.

Silenus, then, is no ordinary tutor, no ordinary caretaker of children. The job of the normal tutor is to shepherd the child through the process of becoming an adult. The tutor teaches the child about the world that must be inhabited. The tutor builds skills, passes on knowledge, then his work is done. He sends the child off toward life and inevitably toward the death that is final. But Silenus must be the tutor of the life process itself.

That is a strange and overwhelming position. How do you teach life to be life? And is that even what Silenus is really teaching? Dionysus has nothing, actually, to learn. He must simply go through the process of being born and then ripped apart in death again and again as the seasons cycle through, as the rhythm of winter and spring and the harvest cycles through again and again. Dionysus doesn't learn anything so much as make it happen. Or maybe we should say that he is it happening. Dionysus is the god of the happening of life. Thus his infinite and near complete muteness. Dionysus says nothing and has nothing to say. He can have nothing to say. There is nothing to be said.

Silenus is tutor and attendant to the mute god, the god to whom nothing can be said and nothing can be learned. And the drunkenness of Silenus comes out of that. This is the drunkenness that Rubens captures in his painting. It is not the drunkenness of revelry or even of manic frenzy. Silenus is not frenzied in Rubens's painting. He isn't taking part in the bacchanalian revelry. If anything, he stumbles away from the goings-on. He wants to be elsewhere, except that there is nowhere else to be. In his drunkenness, he would stumble outside of the painting altogether.

He would join us in death. He would join the mortal throng. That is one great insight of Rubens's painting, isn't it? That Silenus would join the rest of us in a mortal death. That his wisdom, given to King Midas in all its harsh brutality is, in fact, a secret blessing. The best thing for man, Silenus is telling King Midas, is that you get to die. You get to die.

"Would that I could die with you."

"I do not seek to die with you," says Silenus secretly, "because of my suffering, but because it is the only thing that makes the suffering worthwhile."

"I seek the suffering unto death," says Silenus, "the one thing I cannot have."

That is something Nietzsche didn't see, couldn't see. Nietzsche thought that the joke was on man. Nietzsche thought that Silenus looks with contempt upon man. Rubens thinks that Silenus looks upon man with sad envy. Silenus would take it upon himself to become man, if only he could do that. He would take up the flesh and see it wither. He would go into death. But Silenus cannot do that, because he is the tutor to life and death itself. He is trapped in the meta-process. His drunkenness is the grasping at an oblivion that will not come. The indifference of Dionysus is beyond him because he is so much closer to man. So close to man, he almost grasps death, but cannot. He stumbles toward it in his drunkenness. He stumbles toward us wanting to be one with our flesh. He is neither here nor there in his drunken stumbling.

Nietzsche couldn't see what Rubens saw in Silenus because he wouldn't. Nietzsche wanted a philosophy of life in its full brutality. He wanted an affirmation of life that presented life as sheer discharge. Nietzsche had the courage to give up on metaphysics. He had the courage to take life as sheer discharge and nothing more. I will take the sheer discharge he said. He was willing to say yes to the discharge. That is the courage of Nietzsche. He thought of Silenus as the first prophet of life as a sheer discharge. He thought that Silenus spoke to King Midas in order to let the world of mortals know that life is sheer discharge, that it can be put into the sound of the goat bleating in the forest. The cry of a goat god in the forest running after the trail of a nymph. The terrible and beautiful noises of the goat in its act of passion and discharge. The rape of the girl. The murder of the goat. The goat fucks and dies. The bleating echoes through the forest and then is silenced. Sheer discharge. That is what Silenus speaks of like a prophet, thought Nietzsche. Silenus, thought Nietzsche, is the prophet of the goat god and the sheer discharge of life.

But that isn't what Rubens saw at all. Rubens saw something else in the drunken stumbling of the Silenus. He sees Silenus with compassion. Compassion? No one thinks of Rubens as a painter of compassion. He is a painter of skill. He is a painter with tremendous theatrical gifts. He is a painter of life and of flesh. He is a painter we would expect, with Nietzsche, to see in Silenus the prophet of sheer discharge. But he does not. He does not paint Silenus that way. He shows us a Silenus in his struggling and stumbling who would become one with man, a being-toward-death along with the rest of us. Rubens shows us a drunken immortal who would give anything to participate in the world we have been given, the brief and seemingly meaningless world of mortal existence.

17. The lessons of Jan Rubens are the lessons that can only be passed down in silence.

JAN RUBENS, THE FATHER OF PETER PAUL Rubens, our painter, died in the year 1587. Peter Paul Rubens would have been ten years old, then, when his father died. He would never even have had the opportunity to speak directly of serious things with his father. It can be difficult enough for any of us to speak of serious things with our fathers, at any age. Who is able, really, to understand the life of the father as a life? Who can ever see their father as a man and not as a father? But a boy of ten years old definitely cannot do that. Peter Paul Rubens cannot have done that. His father would have died as a father to Peter Paul Rubens, not as a man.

But there must have been transferences all the same. In ten years, much would have been transferred. Feelings and attitudes would have been transferred from father to son. All the sadnesses of the father, all the things he lost. The broken man may have had a way of talking, he may have had a way simply of sitting in his chair that conveyed real experience. This is a man, remember, who ran openly toward death, who courted the abyss. He grabbed the hand of Anna of Saxony and he went to death with abandon. And then he reduced himself to a vapor and returned to his wife in broken shame. He abandoned everything he had known and returned to his wife as a supplicant. And then she wrote him that incredible and terrible letter. He was forced to read that letter again and again, if only in his mind.

That was the household in which Peter Paul Rubens came to be a person. He would have watched his father in his daily affairs. He would have seen his father in his daily interactions. He would have caught his father, sometimes, sitting alone on a chair in one of the family rooms, staring off into space and thinking about the past. He would have absorbed, without knowing exactly what was happening, the things of his father.

The details don't matter at all. It doesn't matter whether Peter Paul Rubens knew the details of his father's life or his mother's life. None of the specifics can be important at all in relation to the moment that can be imagined in which an eight-year-old Peter Paul Rubens is sitting on a stairway looking through the wooden balustrade at his father in a chair in the room below. It is morning or whatever. Who cares? A morning light of this or that quality is streaming gently through the glass of the late-sixteenth-century windows. Let it be like that. We don't care very much. We know how mottled and bubbly that old glass can be, that sixteenth-century glass, blown back in the days before they had all the techniques for industrial glassblowing and refining. It would have looked like a Vermeer painting, maybe, that scene between Rubens the father and Rubens the son. Rubens the father would have been unaware that he is being observed just at that moment by Rubens the son, sitting on the stairway and watching the light come in through the windows of late-sixteenth-century glass. Imagine it to be however you like, it doesn't matter.

The fact is that these two people actually existed, once. It is almost impossible to make that thought real. But it must be real. These two people actually existed as flesh and blood human beings in the real world. Jan Rubens was a man. He gave birth to a son. These two human beings lived in a house together in the town of Siegen in what is now modern-day Germany. They lived together as father and son for ten years until the day that Jan Rubens died. For ten years a small and growing boy had every opportunity to watch the man. He would have watched the man, alright. We have the paintings painted by the man that the boy later became. We know that he watched. We know that he observed. We know that he was sensitive to the play of light through those late Renaissance panes of glass.

18. The silence of Jan Rubens is connected by actual, material, long-running historical threads to the silence of The Sea Peoples.

WE KNOW MANY THINGS ABOUT the world within which the lives of the Rubens family made sense. We can run history forward from the religious wars of those times up through Nietzsche at the gates of Metz. And we can run it backward too. We can go back further through the great medieval kingdoms that predate the Houses of the Hapsburgs and the Houses of the Bourbons. We can go back into the very emergence of the medieval world after the breaking apart of the Roman Empire and we can go back before that to the Mediterranean world in which the ancient empires worshiped the Greek gods like Dionysus. We can go back to the period of the great heroes and the myths and legends that Homer sang about. And when we run it all the way back to those times we come up, again, against the black box of the Sea Peoples.

We do not know anything about The Sea Peoples. The Sea Peoples, the ones who ravaged the

Mediterranean world sometime during the thirteenth century BCE, we don't know a thing about them. We only hear about their coming. Then the Mycenaean civilization is gone. Then the Hittite civilization is gone. Then the Egyptian civilization is on the run, retreating to its inland borders.

A few scribes in the Hittite lands of what is now modern Turkey talk about ships appearing. A few ships appear in the harbor. Black ships. And total silence. No one says anything. No demands are made. No envoys are exchanged. There is nothing to be done. The ships arrive. Then, the next day, there are more ships. "Get out of there when you see the first ship," warns the scribe. But where can you go when all of civilization is being ripped apart? There is nowhere else to go.

We don't know what actually happened after the ships came, the ships of The Sea Peoples. All we know is that those cities start being erased from the map. The Sea Peoples were makers of ruins. They were like the pre-forces of archaeology sent back into time. They found civilization and they put it down. They put it down under the earth, to be uncovered later by another time. They didn't build anything, The Sea Peoples. They don't seem to have had the impulse. They were not interested in the game of power and politics. They had no envoys, no emissaries. They didn't want anything. That must have been an incredible thing, to see the ships appearing and to realize that they didn't want anything, nothing that could be put into words. No demands were made. Just a waiting. And then, in silence, the obliteration of civilization all the way down to stones. When The Sea Peoples were done, they had put entire civilizations under the earth, buried them for the distant future to uncover in tiny fragments.

We don't know what language The Sea Peoples spoke, because they left no documents. They had nothing at all, except those ships, described by at least one scribe of the time as being black. They had black ships that are long since decomposed in the corrosive waters of the Mediterranean. They came into history to make ruins, to cancel history, and then they dissolved into it themselves. They wanted nothing, had nothing to say, nothing to make, nothing to give. In purity, they destroyed. In silence. If you want The Sea Peoples to speak you are going to be disappointed. They are the most consistent people in the entirety of human history. The Sea Peoples had complete and total disbelief in history. They did not destroy civilization in order to participate in the story of civilization. They came to cancel history, to push it under. They are completely consistent in this regard. If The Sea Peoples had things their way, there would have been no more history. That is why they had nothing to say. There was no one to say it to. They came in order to cancel the story. The only way to cancel the story is to do it in silence. The Sea Peoples came with a giant silence, a silence big enough to mute civilization, a silence big enough to suppress history.

There is no history in this part of the world after The Sea Peoples, not for a long time. For all practical purposes, there is no history for the century or two that comes after The Sea Peoples. They did it. In silence, they came in their black ships and canceled everything down to the very bone. The mute people from the sea, the most consistent people who ever lived on this planet yet.

For centuries there is nothing. A wasteland. A gap in the story, a tear in the fabric of history. And then, on the ruins of the Mycenaean civilization that had been wiped away by The Sea Peoples, on the piles of meaningless stones that had been the Hittite civilization something new finally started to assert itself. King Midas started to piece a civilization back together. He discovered a wealth of gold in the rivers and he began to extend the boundaries of civilization again. He suspected that something had been lost; he saw the old ruins. He was greedy for the old secrets and the lost stories when everything was cut down to the bone by The Sea Peoples. He went out into the forest, finally, because he had heard of Silenus. He had heard that the Silenus could be found in the forest and that the Silenus was in possession of actual wisdom, that he could say something true about man and what is best for man. So King Midas went looking for that. Out of history's cancelation at the hands of The Sea Peoples, King Midas went looking for Silenus and the oldest pieces of wisdom in order to put things back together again.

19. There is a great and nameless wisdom to be found in the murky space between life and death, the space from which silence speaks.

IS SILENUS ALIVE? THAT IS A STRANGE question, I know. He is most obviously a living man the way Rubens paints him. But in a way he is not alive, since he cannot die. Dionysus is a god and will continue the process of being born in the ritual and being torn apart in the ritual and being reborn again forever. There is no great sense in asking whether Dionysus is alive since he transcends all that. Dionysus, if he is anything, is the process of life in itself and so he is one level beyond the level at which one actually lives. He looks over life and death. You could say that Dionysus exists, maybe. He exists because life and death exist. You could look at it that way. You could say that Dionysus exists and that that existence is permanent insofar as life and death continue to happen. As long as there are creatures going through the process of life and death, then there is Dionysus.

And as long as there is Dionysus, there is Silenus. So in that way, Silenus exists. He has an existence

There is a great and nameless wisdom to be found that is attached to the existence of Dionysus. But he isn't really alive, since he does not, will not, cannot experience death. Silenus needs to be around to take care of Dionysus every time he is torn apart and then put back together again as the child god. That condition is permanent. Dionysus is always, at every moment, in the process of manifesting his nature as the man god and as the child god. He is always being torn apart and he is always being put back together again. And Silenus is always there as the shepherd of Dionysus's boyish nature, the side of him that can be born anew at every moment. Silenus does not get to exit this process.

But more than Dionysus, whose relationship to life is entirely of a second order nature, Silenus achieves a measure of life. He seems to be living a life as he trudges around attending to the boyhood needs of Dionysus into infinity. Perhaps that also accounts for the infinite nature of his tiredness. Titian doesn't, and Rubens certainly doesn't, portray Silenus as the energetic Dionysian in the midst of a frenzy. The Maenads are portrayed that way. The satyrs and the nymphs are portrayed that way. It was obvious to Rubens that many of the characters riding around with Dionysus ought to be portrayed as energetic, as fully engaged in the process of living in its abundance. The drunkenness of the satyrs and nymphs is the drunkenness of excess. This is the drunkenness of overflow. Plus, there is the fucking. The drunkenness around Silenus is marked by the drunkenness of abandon, of the about-to-be-fucked and those who are going to fuck them.

The Drunken Silenus

Silenus is different, though. His drunkenness isn't connected to abundance or to abandon. His drunkenness doesn't connect him to life in the way that it expresses or overflows. Silenus's drunkenness pushes him to the margins, to the shadows. It puts him in the gray space between life and death. His drunkenness is slow and ponderous and obscured by mists. He is walking through a hazy and indeterminate landscape, like a place in the netherworld. At the very least, he is a creature, this drunken Silenus, of the threshold. You can imagine him dwelling in a space just between life and death, a place that is neither and both.

That is probably the reason Rubens looked at the painting by Titian and got rid of Dionysus altogether. The way Dionysus leaps down from his chariot upon Ariadne—it has the stench of playacting about it. Dionysus isn't leaping into the real world, after all. He isn't really leaping into life. He isn't leaping into love. How can he love Ariadne, anyway? She is an insect to him. She is already dead. In the infinite scope of Dionysus, she has flitted away into ashes in the time that he bats an eye. A glance from one side to the other might as well count for a millennium from the perspective of Dionysus. A nod of his head could encompass the duration in which a thousand generations of living beings come to be and pass away. A generation of men grow old and die as Dionysus checks his fingernails or lets a thought cloud and then dissipate in his mind.

Homer was trying to express something like this when he described the head of Zeus nodding in assent

There is a great and nameless wisdom to be found in that passage of *The Iliad*. "And with blue-black brows the son of Kronos nodded, and the ambrosial locks of the ruler flowed, waving from his immortal head; he shook great Olympus." A slow turn of his head and the whole world shakes. Suddenly the immensity of the idea strikes you in that passage from Homer. Zeus is not a person so much as a force. The Divine is there. Or what is it?

You have to think of Dionysus like that, like Zeus turning his head that shakes worlds, when you see Dionysus as beyond life and death. His existence is the existence that manifests the essence of life and death. And then to see him leaping out of his chariot like a pretty prince, it all seems like so much playacting. If you understood Dionysus through Titian's painting you could be forgiven for suspecting that Ariadne hangs herself from that tree out of sheer disappointment. The god manifested and it was only that, only the leaping lad of the chariot? Titian hasn't grasped the full import of Dionysus and his confrontation with Ariadne in his painting. He has missed something.

In fact, it is Ariadne's hanging of herself from a tree that brings her closer to Silenus. It was not Titian's leaping lad of the chariot that Ariadne saw. Instead, we should understand that Ariadne does get a glimpse of the true, the awesome, the unseeable. The divine does come to her in some way that we cannot even imagine, that for which we do not have words or pictures. Do not look upon the face of God, for you cannot bear it. But she does. Ariadne, for whatever reason, gets a glimpse.

The divine reveals itself to her and that revelation rips open the fabric of her finitude. She cannot be the creature that she was before. Like Silenus, she has been brought to the threshold. She has seen something a little bit beyond life and a little bit beyond death. She cannot get back into the world again after that. Not properly. She isn't attached to the world properly anymore. She starts to see little rips in the fabric of the world around her. After that, life seems to her only an illusion or, by turns, too real to be borne. She can't bear it. That can happen when you get a glimpse of the Divine, when the fabric tears. Finally, the only way to be alive again would be to die. The terrible paradox of Ariadne. She has her mortality. The only thing that could possibly save her is her mortality, which she must die in order to experience. She realizes that the only way to come back into the world again would be to die. She gets a rope and she ties it into a noose. She climbs into the branches of her tree. Because of her desire to come back to the world after having glimpsed the Divine, she kills herself, hanging herself from the branches of that tree.

* * *

Silenus can't hang himself, though. It doesn't work for him, couldn't work for him. He would just hang there, presumably, until one of the satyrs came to get him down. They would put him back on the ass and ride off into the forest toward the next bacchanal. Silenus could dangle from every olive tree in Greece and still

There is a great and nameless wisdom to be found

the Dionysian retinue would gather him up again for the next round of revelry.

Silenus is living a kind of life, but he doesn't get the full smack of mortal experience. Without the mortality, life isn't real enough to be the real thing. That's why, in Rubens's version of Silenus, he couldn't possibly be a participant in the festivities. He doesn't feel the pull of it. He doesn't have the aching need that you can hear in the bleat of those goats. The bleat of the goat is a life-cry and it surely has something to do with the fucking. The potential for violence and for running you-know-not-where in the forest can be heard in the bleat of the goat. That noise doesn't mean much for Silenus anymore. Imagine that he has heard it a million times over a thousand life cycles. What could it mean to him anymore except for the infinite tedium of repetition? Repetition again and again and then again all over.

Have you ever seen a goat in the forest? Suddenly it lets out that noise and its body leaps up, all four legs, and it hurls itself to one side or another. They leap up, goats do, out of nowhere and toward nothing. They don't care. They make a noise and then jettison themselves this way and that. The bleating is upon them, the forest need. Silenus doesn't care about that anymore, even though he endures it. He endures just enough of it to be a part, but not enough to be a full participant. He is there and not there. And always drinking, always drinking himself into the gray area of consciousness. That is the zone where Rubens paints him with his massive knobby knees and his forward trudging through the haze at the threshold.

He has just come back, Silenus has, from his brief incarceration and interrogation at the hands of King Midas. King Midas asked him what the best thing for man was. Put all of the carefulness and the niceties of King Midas's question aside. What is King Midas really getting at? What did he really want to know? Really, King Midas wanted to know about death. He wanted to know how to transcend death. He wanted a trick by which he could get out of the cycle, by which he could be above death. He wanted to cheat death by any means possible, did King Midas. He wanted to live on and on. He realizes that his own death will make all of his power and all of his desire pointless. He decides that death is the problem. He wouldn't have this emptiness if not for the surety of death. So, King Midas prefers to live. That is his preference. That is the real desire hiding behind his question. He dresses the question up in fine language about the best thing for man. But he doesn't even know what that means, the best thing for man. Really he wants to know the secret of death, the ultimate thing. He wants to live past the allotted time in spirit or in body, preferably in body.

Silenus sniffs out the real intent of the question. He knows the pain of living. He hears the bleat of the goat every day in the forest and knows something of the unnamable desires that give vent to it. The bleat comes up from a deep place and from a dark place. Silenus knows that. He knows that King Midas wants to live

There is a great and nameless wisdom to be found

on and on. So he tells King Midas the truth. Death is actually a gift. But you can't see the gift as the gift that it actually is. You've been given a gift and you want more than anything to throw the thing away. Don't throw it away. Run to it if you can. Be the life-toward-death that you are. Silenus takes the real question hidden inside the fake question of King Midas and brings it to the surface, lays it bare.

From his shadow existence he speaks a truth that is not a shadow at all. It is clear and bright.

20. If Jan Rubens came to know anything, he came to know the threshold. And his son saw the threshold in him and wanted to know the threshold too.

THERE IS THEN, AFTER ALL, A SILENUS in the shadow-man of Jan Rubens, the man who ran toward death and was turned away at the threshold. What kind of world did Jan inhabit for those final years after he received the letter from his wife, Maria, and in the years before death finally did take him away in a second dispensation? He inhabited a Silenusian world, of course. He wandered around in the shadows that Silenus knew and that Ariadne would have known after her disastrous and unwanted encounter with the Divine in the leap of Dionysus. This is a world in which death hovers and in which life hovers but in which neither of them give anything solid. It is the land of the threshold, where nothing is real.

Jan Rubens lived his life once and then he had to live a second version of it in the shadow land of a partial death. He had to live a second life under the shadow of that letter from Maria Rubens, the letter that reduced him to a vapor and gave him another existence in the vaporous and misty realm of the threshold.

If you can think of Jan Rubens as having received a small gift once he was reduced to vapors, then you can see him as living that brief second life in some gratitude. He would have learned something in his reduction. He would have come to the core truth of himself after everything else was burned away. It was burned away for Jan Rubens. That much we know. It was burned away and Jan Rubens was forced to live with what was left, which cannot have been much.

Or maybe it was. Maybe the tiny truth that was left to Jan Rubens after everything else was burned away was a precious thing after all. He wouldn't have needed or wanted to tell anyone else about it. He was done with all that. He was done with talking. He was done with running, running toward death or anything else. We don't have much access to the truth that was available to Jan Rubens after he was burned into vapors and then forced to confront whatever was left. The truth that was available to Jan Rubens in the final years of his life, after the prison in Germany at the hands of William the Silent, would have been something that he knew and understood through his experience. It would have been the thing that sustained him in the shadow world as he raised his young children in his zone on the cusp between life and death.

21. A painter comes to know the cracks in reality.

DOES A PAINTING CREATE A SECOND world, a shadow world? It is another world, at least. The frame does that right away, the borders of the painting make it happen. The borders of the painting become the borders of a second world. The painting is on the inside and the real world is on the outside. You make a painting to connect to the world, but then you've accidentally created a second world that lurks in shadow and ambiguity. What is it? What is its reality? Does it have reality? When you get to the edges of the painting, you must wonder, what do I do at the edges here? The edges bring up the problem. How does this world inside the painting relate to the other world that I inhabit?

You end up spending a lot of time there in that alternate world when you are a painter. You end up inhabiting that second world. It isn't a world of life and it isn't a world of death. It is, though, another world. It doesn't exist in the way that the world of life exists, that is certain. The world of the painting is a world without movement in space or time. The things that happen inside a painting happen within the logic of that inner world. The events of a painting don't unfold over time the way that events of the world do. They happen all at once, in the arrangement of elements that are otherwise static within the painting. There is quite a lot happening, for instance, in Rubens's painting of the drunken Silenus. But it isn't happening in the way that events in the real world are happening, it isn't happening sequentially; it is happening all at once and forever.

Still, when you spend a lot of time inside the world of a painting, when, for instance, you are painting that painting, you must become, over time, comfortable with the logic of the way things happen in that world, in the world of the painting. It is a second existence and you, the painter, go into that existence and then come out of it.

A painting is also supposed to relate to the world outside its boundaries, beyond its frame. It is supposed to have an inner logic, it is supposed to make sense within the confines of its own borders, and it is supposed to carry something outside of those boundaries into the world that exists beyond the frame of the painting. So the painter and the painting are both in a tricky position. The second world of the painting involves a double existence. The painter makes a second world and then goes into that world. He goes out again too. He is constantly shifting, the painter, in and out of different forms of existence. A painting is the result of that shifting.

That is why, maybe, Rubens liked to include at least one figure staring straight out of the painting into the world of the viewer. He does it with the painting of the two satyrs that can be viewed at that museum in Germany. The one satyr stares straight at us from the painting. He directs his wicked gaze directly at us. Rubens enjoyed painting figures who look at us directly from out of the painting. He does the same thing in the painting with Silenus. We, the viewers, are being addressed, but even more than that, the very fact that the boundary between the world of the painting and the real world is being leapt over is addressed.

The figures that look out from Rubens's paintings look out in full knowledge that they are looking out. That feeling is usually heightened by the contrast. I mean that there is usually, in Rubens's paintings that contain such a figure, at least one figure who is fully within the space, the world, of the painting and who isn't looking out, and then there is one figure who has moved out of that space, who draws attention to the fact that there is an inside and an outside to the painting. In the painting of the two satyrs it is important, you see, that the one satyr in the back is fully concentrated on sipping his wine. He is completely within the space of the painting. I mean that he is living within that world. He is wrapped up in it. He sips his wine and looks down at the cup. Some of the wine is dribbling out of the left side of his mouth, the side that is revealed to us. His right hand, holding the cup, is almost like a protective barrier against the frame of the painting further to the left. That satyr is enclosed on himself, within the world of the painting, you could say. He doesn't even need the arbitrary enclosure of the frame. He is making a frame with his own body. He is the frame. In contrast to that, the satyr in front, the primary satyr is facing right at us. He's all opened up, as it were. His shoulders are open. His face is open. His right hand is caught midway in the process of bringing a bunch of grapes up to his mouth. He was going to take a big bite of grapes. But he stops. What's that? He has just noticed something. There are two worlds. He sees that fact, he knows it. He is aware, suddenly, that there is another world. He makes us aware of the fact that he is aware.

"Holy shit," he says, "you're out there and I'm in here and we both know it. This whole thing is a joke."

The whole act of painting is a joke and we all pretend it isn't a joke and a trick but, then again, the joke is also pretty damn serious in that it's a joke and a trick that reveals something, that reveals the shadowy nature of reality itself. The false reality of the painting isn't, therefore, so false at all. The false reality of the painting shows us something about the true nature of the presumptive real reality.

So Rubens had a reason for painting in this way. The strange and otherworldly ability to occupy the threshold between life and death in the act of painting was a revelation to him. He wanted to show figures looking out from his paintings, maybe, because the experience was powerful to him. He was obsessed with the two worlds. He was obsessed with the fact that while he painted he was constantly traveling from the shadow world of the painting into the real world upon which the painting is dependent and that, finally, in all the transition, the very meaning of reality would sometimes dissolve for him. Sometimes, it probably even struck him that the painting world could seem more real than the real world. Sometimes he may have been dizzied by the experience. He could have wondered what is really real. He could have wondered if we have it right. He could have wondered whether shadows have more truth than what seems so clear in the light of day.

The nymph who looks out at us so knowingly in the Silenus painting is looking at us with the same knowing glance that Rubens would give us were he within the painting. It is the look that knows what is going on and thus erases the boundary between the two worlds. The nymph in the painting of Silenus is looking at us with the gaze of Rubens.

But there is another shadow world, another double world inside the painting as well. Silenus, in Rubens's painting, has no idea that he is inside a painting. The nymph knows it—she draws attention to the boundary between the painting and the real world by looking directly into our eyes, the viewers who are viewing the painting. But Silenus can't look at anyone, either within the painting or without. He is playing the role, within Rubens's painting, of the sipping satyr in the two satyrs painting. Silenus, like the sipping satyr, is oblivious to the boundary, oblivious to the fact that he is operating in a two-worlds scenario. Except that in his act of drunkenness, Silenus is, in his own way, moving toward a threshold and bringing himself into a space between life and death. Silenus is no longer sensible within the world of the painting. He has lost his sense in there.

Look again at the way the black satyr is pinching at his flesh, the flesh on the lower left thigh of Silenus. It is a good pinch, hard. It is the kind of pinch that a person in their normal senses would respond to with a start. But Silenus doesn't respond. He simply surges forward. Inertia, the special inertia of drunkenness, has taken hold over his entire being. His right leg is practically dragging along. The top of his right foot is scraping across the ground. He can't even get his feet into the proper position for normal walking. Physiologically, Rubens is giving us the study of a person insensible, insensate, out of his senses. He is drunk, after all. Extremely drunk. Silenus is so drunk that a vicious ass-pinch has no effect on him at all. He has drunk himself beyond the point of even noticing that a chunk of his ass is practically coming off in that pinch. But he hasn't quite drunk himself out of the painting and into the real world. Maybe the painting would dump him into the real world, what with its tilt and its movement toward the bottom left hand of the painting. But even if it did, Silenus would not know the difference. He is stumbling toward a third alternative. He is oblivious both to the world of the painting that he is within, and the real world that the nymph becomes aware of with her gaze. Silenus is entering a world that is neither here nor there.

This was the purpose, of course, of all the drinking around Dionysius and the Dionysian rites in the first place. Alcohol has magical properties. It takes you away from your normal sensations. It removes a person from the order of reality that one normally knows. In terms of the Dionysian rites, this allowed for the possibility of coming into communion with something beyond life in its day-to-day existence. Being drunk in the Dionysian rites allowed for the possibility of acting differently. In point of fact, the drunkenness would allow for excess and for revelry. It does not take a great degree of imagination to imagine the possibilities for fucking and for fighting that arise within the drunken gatherings of Dionysius. Life in the mode of the goat is immediate. You might find yourself fucking or fighting at any moment. The goat will spring into the air and utter one of its guttural bleats. The goat-man, the satyr, runs off into the forest in pursuit of another nymph, who will be tracked down and taken by force.

The drunkenness also allows for the rites themselves, the terrible rites in which living things will be sacrificed in ritual play around the death and eventual rebirth of Dionysius. A goat or some other animal will be hacked into pieces after it has been tricked into giving its assent by means of a shiver or some other sign. The sacred priests of the rite pour some cold water onto the goat and the goat shakes and shivers. The priests of the Dionysian rite interpret the sign of the goat. The goat is ready to die and will be killed right there at the center of the rite. It will be cooked up in the triple-legged cauldron where floats some other meat, some unknown meat that may be that of a child, that is supposed, at least, to make reference to the actual sacrifice of Dionysius as the child. Is human meat ever used? Was it ever used up there in the Greek mountains where they practiced the secret rites in their caves and grottoes? It is not known. Through it all, the drinking of alcohol brings one past the limits of daily life and the prescriptions and limitations of daily life. The drunkenness brings the wildness out and the wildness allows for the killing and the expression of pure excess.

But one of the participants is not like that. Silenus is not like that. He doesn't drink in order to lower his inhibitions and to take part in the Dionysian frenzy. Silenus drinks in order to bring himself into the gray area between life and death, the very place he must inhabit as the caretaker of Dionysius. Silenus cannot be of life since he cannot die. Silenus cannot be dead since he is connected to life. He has a life that is not a life; a living death that is not death at all.

22. The truth of all art is, ultimately, the truth of finitude, or the truth of passing away, a passing truth. Or something like that.

IT MUST CREATE A STRANGE SENSATION indeed, to know in all likelihood that you are painting a painting whose existence will out-exist you, the painter. It is often said that one motivation for the production of art, at least from the artist's perspective, is the promise of immortality. The old poets would talk about this openly sometimes.

"Would that this little book last forever," Catullus writes in his book of poems.

He is laughing, but the little book does just that. There is something funny in the wish of Catullus since his poems are, for the most part, so small, so personal, so particular that they would seem to be the very opposite of that which lasts. In another of his poems, Catullus mourns the death of his lover's sparrow as if it were the death of a king. He is playing, having fun with the contrast.

"Mourn, ye gods!" Catullus proclaims, "mourn the death of my lady's sparrow."

The truth of all art is, ultimately, the truth of finitude

Catullus is amused by the contrast between the bigness of his feelings and the littleness of the occasion. This is the very same attitude that he directs toward his little book of poems that he would send into eternity. It is a strange thing to wish eternity upon poems that resolutely refuse to speak to the ages. Catullus seems to have known there was something funny about this even as he writes it. There is a mock grandiosity to his tone, to Catullus's attitude as he calls out for the ages to come and carry his poems into immortality. Yet the ages do come and do just that. And Catullus seems to have known it would happen. He seems to have understood and mastered the paradox, somehow. He seems to have grasped that the wish for immortality has to be wrapped up within the embrace of mortality for the whole thing to pull itself off. You must praise sparrows and meaningless afternoon fucking. You must embrace the small scraps of time if you want to be large enough to last for ages.

One wonders, then, whether Catullus was ever angry at his poems for their potential to realize an immortality that was unavailable to Catullus in his lifetime. What is so great, you could ask, about having created something that will live on past your own death? Isn't such an achievement merely a confirmation of the finality of the demise that the achievement was supposed, somehow, to mock? That is the best you can do to cheat death? That's all we have available to us? King Midas would not have been impressed with the promise of immortality that requires the death of the person and the eternal life of a poem, or a painting. That kind of immortality would only seem to prove the absolute and complete victory of death. The triumph over death that is supposed to be the result of art would be nothing more than the complete capitulation to death. Catullus's poems ask to be remembered for eternity, and then they speak of the deaths of little birdies belonging to Roman girls and also, much of the time, of the weariness and the compulsion involved with fucking and with being fucked.

One could suppose that Rubens was completely aware of this problem in his paintings. There is no life in these objects I've painted, he would have thought. And there is no death either. In painting, I carry myself into an immortality that is empty and gray, a threshold space where permanent existence is achieved at the cost of reality. The very painting that Rubens painted is, then, formally and in its subject matter, a lament about eternity and death. Rubens painted the way that Silenus existed. It is a lament about eternity and death. But not just a lament. A promise. Death is the only answer. Death, somehow, is an answer.

23. Silenus, the deathless one who yearns for death, is thus the truth of all art. It's just funny that this truth comes in the form of a drunken fat man.

A WOMAN BLOCKS THE PASSAGE Silenus would take in his drunken stumbling. We haven't spoken about this woman yet. She is grotesque. She is naked and hunched over with her right arm drooping down toward the ground, flopping down, really. Her face is puffy and insensible. She is, like Silenus, and unlike the nymphs and satyrs, drunk in the way that has carried her into the no-man's land of emptiness and confusion. Two baby satyrs, two fat little beasts are lying on the ground and nursing from her breasts in an upside-down manner. They are really tugging at her. Her right breast is stretched to what seems like a painful degree by the greedy little satyr lying on that side. But, like Silenus getting the hard pinch from the black satyr, she is oblivious to the sensation. She is past sensation and she has entered into the netherworld.

The Drunken Silenus

The netherworld is the place of drunkenness that is one step past the threshold. The drunken nymph on the ground being sucked on by the young satyrs is beyond the possibility of experiencing a double world. She is gone completely. She has become the source, quite literally, of the nectar that sustains the satyrs in their world. They are suckling at her breasts, after all. It is not hard to imagine that the milk coming from this nymph is highly intoxicating. She is sauced up and she is passing that sauce on to the little satyrs. So there is the self-enclosed and cyclical world of the satyrs and their constant dance around Dionysus right there. From the perspective of the nymphs and the satyrs and of Dionysus himself the cycle of birth and death is infinite, eternal, and without interruption.

This nymph lying on the ground and allowing the little satyrs to suckle from her breasts is blocking the way of Silenus. He will, presumably, trip over her or otherwise come into contact with her as an impediment. So, the black satyr is pinching Silenus and sending him careening toward the threshold of the painting and presumably toward a possible breach of that threshold (note, again, the tipped-over, downward spill of the painting's orientation) while the nursing nymph on the ground is blocking the otherwise out-of-the-painting trajectory of Silenus as he stumbles along in his own semi-stupor.

Silenus is caught between escaping the painting and not escaping the painting. That condition of being between escape and captivity is not unlike the condition in which Silenus finds himself in the myth. Silenus is, after all, somewhere between dying and not dying. He is not fully immortal like Dionysus, he isn't a true god, nor is he fully mortal like King Midas, since he must always exist in order to be the attendant of Dionysus as Dionysus is perennially born and then torn apart and then reborn and then torn apart again. And Silenus is also, we should mention again, extremely drunk in the painting. And one of the key aspects of being very drunk, as everyone knows, is that you are conscious without being all the way conscious. You are there without being all the way there. You are present while at the same being absent. You are moving around without going anywhere.

The nymph on the ground with the greedy, monstrous baby satyrs is the closed circle of the Dionysian cycle. She will not let Silenus out of the painting. She will not let him be incarnated. She will not let him take on the flesh, to live so that he may die, and to die so that he may live. Silenus will stay in the shadow lands.

24. The truth of finitude must itself be finite, subject to obliteration.

IT IS THOUGHT BY MANY THAT PETER Paul Rubens never knew anything about the story of his father's run toward death with Anna of Saxony and subsequent humiliation until after his father's death. During the years in Siegen, Germany (or what was to become Germany only during Nietzsche's time) the Rubens family lived modestly and only at the pleasure of William the Silent. Jan Rubens was under a house arrest of sorts. Vast amounts of money were owed to William the Silent as punishment for the crimes of adultery that Jan had committed. The Rubens family would have scratched out an existence under house arrest. They were looking for ways to get money from relatives and anyone who might have owed something to Jan Rubens during the days when he was a more prominent man and a lawyer and person of political influence in Antwerp. But they had nothing. Jan Rubens would never have anything again, no worldly goods or prestige. He would die a broken and forgotten man.

Peter Paul Rubens knew nothing of these details, though. That's what we are led to believe by various letters between Peter and his brother Philip and between other members of the Rubens family later, after the death of Jan. For ten years, more or less. Maria and Jan Rubens lived under house arrest at Siegen after the near-execution of Jan and the letters sent to William the Silent to plead for the life of Jan and the letters between Jan and Maria in which it was made clear that Maria had found within herself deep resources of forgiveness that were beyond what either of them could have any reason to expect and beyond what any person could expect from another person ever. For ten years they lived in those conditions and during the early childhood of Peter Paul those were simply the conditions of his life. He was not aware of the circumstances of their life in Siegen. He was not aware that his father was confined to that house on pain of death. He was not aware that the family was surviving by means of begging and borrowing and making do so that the onerous payments to the House of Orange could be met, ensuring that Jan would not be taken back into prison.

Tensions must have existed in that house. But also, that house may have contained a kind of secret bliss. Anyway, we know nothing about those years. For all practical purposes, those years are ripped out of the knowable part of history. They are a blank place. We know the circumstances. We know the basic conditions under which the Rubens household was living. But a historical fog has settled down into those years. We cannot see into that house. We can see nothing. This opacity is all the more complete for the fact that Siegen does not, today, bear much continuity with the Siegen of the past.

Sliding the history forward from the time of Rubens and through the wars of the House of Orange and the Thirty Years' War and then through the Napoleonic Wars until, finally, we reach the time of Nietzsche and the establishment of the empire of Germany and then reach further beyond that until the struggles between the nation state of France and the nation state of Germany resolve into the First World War and then into the Second World War, we eventually reach the moment when Siegen, home to an important railway connection and close to industrial factories of the Third Reich, is bombed repeatedly by the Allied forces. Something around 3,770 tons of bombs were dropped on Siegen and it was, for all practical purposes, erased from the map as a city. Siegen was rebuilt, of course, after World War II. It was rebuilt, as were so many German cities of that region, as a city that bears only a superficial resemblance to the city that once called itself the home of the Rubens family. Whatever traces left from the days when the Rubens family inhabited Siegen were effectively erased from the historical record. We can never know anything concrete about that decade when the young Peter Paul Rubens was raised from infancy and Jan Rubens lived in the vapors of his shadow existence.

We cannot ever know, for sure, if there was a reprieve for Jan Rubens in those lost days of his final years. It would not have been the reprieve he might have expected when he was running after Anna of Saxony in a mutual dash for the abyss. He was not looking for quiet then, or repose. He was not expecting to be reduced to a vapor and then rekindled from a wisp back into a man again. We don't know what that experience was like for him. We do know that the life of the Rubens family becomes very, very quiet in the decade or so spent in the small city of Siegen, a city that was eventually, though it was impossible for the Rubens family to know this, to be blown up completely, leveled by fleets of flying machines that could drop ton after ton of bombs on the earth far below as they drifted across the sky.

How could the Rubens family have known that the silence of those years immediately after Jan Rubens's release from prison would be given its final seal and sacrament by fleets of flying machines that could drop bombs from thousands of feet in the air? How could the Rubens's family know that the historical events of the religious wars in which they themselves played a part (running the historical story forward through the Napoleonic Wars and the First and the Second Battles of Wörth and then to the great wars of the early twentieth century) would finally result in the burning shut of history and the final closing of those doors of silence? Old Siegen would be bombed off the map. A new Siegen would be built. The silence of the Rubens family and the life in Siegen that was made possible by Maria Rubens's remarkable letter would be made complete by bombs and obliteration. If a shard of the silence exists anywhere it exists on the surfaces of the canvases that Peter Paul Rubens would someday paint, many years after his boyhood in Siegen, Germany. As an adult, Peter Paul Rubens would paint paintings like *The Drunken Silenus* when the memories of a boyhood spent with a shadow-father had faded into tattered and confusing fragments that he himself, surely, never fully understood until his dying day.

25. Weltschmerz.

A FINAL THOUGHT. WHEN THE SEA Peoples came to destroy civilization, when they came to destroy the civilization of the Eastern Mediterranean at the end of the Heroic Age, setting off the Dark Age of the late thirteenth century BCE, when The Sea Peoples brought down the Hittites and the Mycenaeans and reduced civilization back to its bone, they may have been acting from within. The Sea Peoples may simply be the name that a few terrified scribes gave to elements of their own civilizations that had broken off in the chaos of decline and turned against themselves. Maybe, sometimes, civilization wants to go under. It generates its own destructive forces to accomplish that, forces from within that come forth to carry it all under. The record goes black. A moment of total silence when even Silenus can rest.

Further Reading

Friedrich Nietzsche. *The Birth of Tragedy.* The Kaufmann translation is perfectly readable, contrary to many scholarly complaints. The older Vintage edition also includes *The Case of Wagner*, which is nice, and I like the sixties Modernist cover. If you're going to become a Nietzsche scholar you are going to read Nietzsche in the original anyway, so reading a turgid scholarly translation now is of no particular virtue. Also, please, and for God's sake, do not become a Nietzsche scholar.

Michael Fried. *The Moment of Caravaggio.* This book helped me understand certain things about what a painting does in addressing both itself and the viewer. Also, Fried has developed an interesting way of writing art-critical prose, something I'd almost call autistic-poetic.

I never found a biography of Rubens or his time that was much worth reading, I'm sorry. The critical and art historical writing on Rubens is a vast and depressing wasteland. I've read a good chunk of it and do not recommend the experience. The secondary literature on Nietzsche is, also, not very interesting to me. I am, in general, I should say, not against secondary literature. I very much enjoy reading secondary literature and have spent many hours doing it. But in the case of Nietzsche, it is not good. Everyone wants to make of him a specific sort of villain or hero, instead of letting him be the sad little fireball that he actually was.

Roberto Calasso. *The Ruin of Kasch*. Because of a certain way of thinking about history and of civilization. You'll see what I mean.

Martha C. Nussbaum. *The Fragility of Goodness: Luck and Ethics in Greek Tragedy and Philosophy*. It was this book that made me realize how deep is the problem of human sacrifice.

Walter Burkert. *Homo Necans: The Anthropology of Ancient Greek Sacrificial Ritual and Myth*. What, oh Greeks, were you really doing in those caves?

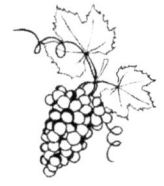

This book was set in Adobe OFL Sorts Mill Goudy,
designed by Barry Schwartz and published by The
League of Moveable Type, the first open-source font
foundry. Based on the classic Goudy Oldstyle, this
typeface retains the strong influence of calligraphy
that characterized its predecessor.

This book was designed by Shannon Carter,
Ian Creeger, and Gregory Wolfe. It was published
in hardcover, paperback, and electronic formats by
Slant Books, Seattle, Washington.

The cover image is a detail from *The Drunken Silenus*,
83.4 x 84.4 inches, oil on panel, 1616–17, and held in the
collection of the Alte Pinakothek, Munich, Germany.

www.ingramcontent.com/pod-product-compliance
Lightning Source LLC
Chambersburg PA
CBHW052239150526
45153CB00030B/336